Making Faces in Fabric

Workshop with Melissa Averinos

Draw, Collage, Stitch & Show

MELISSA AVERINOS

stashBOOKS®

an imprint of C&T Publishing

Text copyright © 2018 by Melissa Averinos

Photography and artwork copyright © 2018 by C&T Publishing, Inc.

PUBLISHER: Amy Marson

CREATIVE DIRECTOR: Gailen Runge

EDITOR: Liz Aneloski

TECHNICAL EDITOR: Debbie Rodgers

COVER/BOOK DESIGNER: April Mostek

PRODUCTION COORDINATOR: Tim Manibusan

PRODUCTION EDITOR: Alice Mace Nakanishi

ILLUSTRATOR: Mary E. Flynn

HAND MODEL: Kristi Visser

PHOTO ASSISTANT: Mai Yong Vang

STYLE PHOTOGRAPHY by Lucy Glover and INSTRUCTIONAL PHOTOGRAPHY by Diane Pedersen of C&T Publishing, Inc., unless otherwise noted

Published by Stash Books, an imprint of C&T Publishing, Inc., P.O. Box 1456, Lafayette, CA 94549

Library of Congress Cataloging-in-Publication Data

Names: Averinos, Melissa, author.

Title: Making faces in fabric : workshop with Melissa Averinos - draw, collage, stitch & show / Melissa Averinos.

Description: Lafayette, California : C&T Publishing, Inc., [2018]

Identifiers: LCCN 2017028921 | ISBN 9781617455445 (soft cover)

Subjects: LCSH: Appliqué--Technique. | Textile crafts. | Face--Miscellanea.

Classification: LCC TT779 .A925 2018 | DDC 746.44/5--dc23

LC record available at https://lccn.loc.gov/2017028921

Printed in China

10 9 8 7 6 5 4 3

DEDICATION As always, this book is dedicated to my adorable husband, Stuart, for believing in me until I believed in myself.

Acknowledgments

I would not be teaching Making Faces had it not been for the encouragement of Penny Layman, who offered me such a fun and forgiving opportunity to try teaching that I couldn't say no. I didn't know how much I would love teaching. Thank you, Penny.

It's a treat to again be working with Roxane Cerda at C&T, who held my hand through my first book-writing experience in 2009. Roxane, thank you for your humor, your friendship, and your confidence in me.

Liz Aneloski at C&T, thank you for taking the reins so gently. You are a dream to work with.

To the Modern Quilt Guild / QuiltCon, all the MQG chapters I've visited, and the students in Making Faces with Melissa classes ... It's through my work with you that I've fine-tuned the process I teach in this book. The excitement I see in your faces when you realize you can do it makes my heart go pitter-patter. (And thanks for all the excellent hugs!)

Most of the art knowledge I have and use every day I learned from my high school art teacher, Carl Lopes. Thank you, Carl, for creating a safe space for a troubled, weird art kid like me—it's the only reason I made it through school.

Thanks to my dad, Tony Averinos, for encouraging my creativity with gifts of art books and supplies all through childhood and since.

Thanks to my mom, Linda Averinos, for letting me raid your craft supplies and draw on the walls.

Thanks to my dear Debbie Kimball, who helps me stay on track in work and in life.

And finally, thanks to my adorable husband, Stuart, for being my rock while I figured all this out. You're the best thing ever and I'm so lucky.

Contents

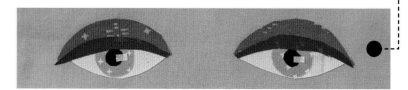

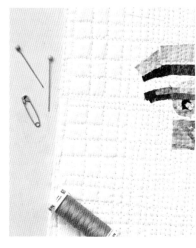

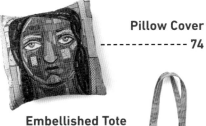

INTRODUCTION

I've been making art since I can remember. When I started painting in middle school, it was always faces. In high school, I continued to explore this theme through self-portraits, glazing pottery with faces, and sculpting clay into little face pendants to use in jewelry. Any medium I tried would soon show someone staring back at me!

It was only a matter of time before this trend would show up in my quilting. After sharing my work on Instagram and exhibiting at QuiltCon, I found that other people wanted to make faces too—and my "Making Faces with Melissa" workshop was born! I now travel all over the country teaching quilters how to make these raw-edge appliqué faces. I love it so much.

People in class are usually intimidated by faces; they are *sure* they won't be able make a decent one. I remind them that they just haven't learned how yet! My favorite thing is seeing people light up when they get it—and they always do. Since not everyone has access to classes, I crammed this book full of my best tips and tricks (and the occasional pep talk), so it will be just like I'm there with you.

In Chapter One: Draw (page 7), you'll learn a simple formula to get the correct proportions of the face and I'll guide you through drawing the features. In Chapter Two: Collage (page 37), I share the basics of collaging with fabric, simple ways to create features, and tips for how to tack them down in preparation for sewing. Then in Chapter Three: Stitch (page 61), you'll learn a handful of stitching options to add texture and secure the fabric.

Once you've spent some time with the technique, check out Chapter Four: Show (page 73), where you'll find a handful of easy projects into which you can incorporate your collage panels. Peruse Chapter Five: Gallery of Author Work (page 87) to see a collection of my quirky faces. And finally, Chapter Six: Gallery of Student Work (page 97) is full of some of the incredible work created in my workshops—many from people with no art experience!

I invite you to approach this book with a willingness to experiment and an attitude of play. The more you can let go and have fun with it, the better your work will be. I'd love it if you would share photos of your collages with me on Instagram (see About the Author, page 111). I can't wait to see the faces you'll make!

Chapter One

Draw

While there are endless variations that make us look different from one another, we all have the same essential facial features. In this chapter, you'll learn how to draw a basic human face, to which you can apply your own artistic style in fabric collage. If you follow these instructions and practice a little, you will be able to draw a face—I promise.

"Before" Drawing

Once you dive into this chapter, you'll learn the basics very quickly. Right now, before you've learned the proportions of the face, I encourage you to take a moment to do a "before" drawing. You won't be able to go back and do this after you've learned some stuff!

To create your "before" drawing, simply grab a plain piece of printer paper, set a timer for 90 seconds, and just draw a face. It may look like a child's drawing and that's perfectly fine! Remember, the worse your "before" looks, the better your "after" will be!

Let's Get Started

What makes a drawing of a face successful is mostly a matter of proportions. Placing the features in the correct spots and making them the right size in relation to one another is the key to drawing a face that looks right.

To get started, you'll need a stack of plain white printer paper, a pencil, and an eraser.

THE MAGIC OF PRINTER PAPER

Though it happens to the best of us, fear of making mistakes is detrimental to creativity. The less precious you can make your process, the more freedom you will feel to mess up or do a "bad job." Making mistakes, learning from them, and correcting them is how you get to the good stuff.

One of the best ways to make drawing less precious is to use plain printer paper instead of a sketchbook. It's liberating to draw on such a cheap and ubiquitous type of paper—you feel totally free to ruin it! If you'd like to keep the pages all together, you can use binder clips, a clipboard, put them in a folder, or use a three-hole punch and keep them in a binder.

DISCLAIMER! Yes, the "basic" face that I base my instructions on is *my own face*! I've always painted self-portraits, so it's the face I know best. Don't worry, I'll give you plenty of tips and options for how to customize your collage to make it look however you like.

PEP TALK

Learning how to draw a face is like going to a new friend's house that you've never been to before, in a town you don't know. At first you may have to drive slowly and pay close attention to the map or directions and you may even make a few wrong turns. After a few times going to the house, you will start to feel more comfortable with the area and you'll know where to go and not need to consult your map. That's how it is with drawing the face. Don't expect it to go perfectly right from the start! You are exploring new territory. Fret not; I've got a good map for you to follow.

It's All about the Proportions

This section guides you through the basic proportions of the head, neck, and ears, as well as guidelines for the placement of the features.

Drawing the Head

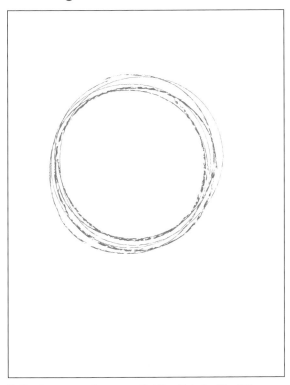

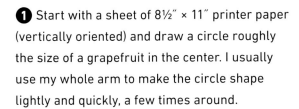

Notice how some lines are slightly off, but with all the light lines combined, it creates a decent circle.

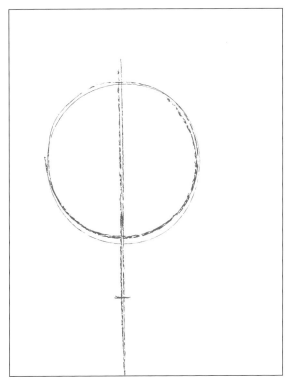

Circle, centerline, and chin marker

❶ Start with a sheet of 8½″ × 11″ printer paper (vertically oriented) and draw a circle roughly the size of a grapefruit in the center. I usually use my whole arm to make the circle shape lightly and quickly, a few times around.

REMINDER This is your last chance to do a "before" drawing! Don't miss the opportunity to record your progress!

❷ Draw a line vertically through the center of the circle all the way down to the bottom of the page.

Now make a little mark where the bottom of the chin will be a little below the bottom of the circle, roughly one-third of the circle's height down.

---

tip *I use cheap plastic mechanical pencils, such as those often given away as a promotional item. I love mechanical pencils because they are always sharp.*

MEASURING TRICK

To help visualize where to put the mark in Step 2 (page 9), here's a little trick. Using your thumb and index finger, gauge the bottom third of the circle. If you place your thumb at the bottom of the circle and your index finger just below the center of the circle, you have a third of the circle between them. Keep that same distance between your fingers and shift your whole hand down so that your index finger is at the bottom of the circle where your thumb was and your thumb is now further down the page, below the circle. That space is roughly the third of the circle.

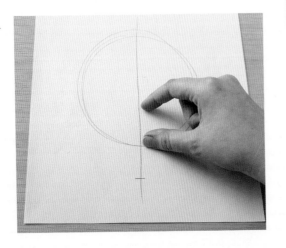

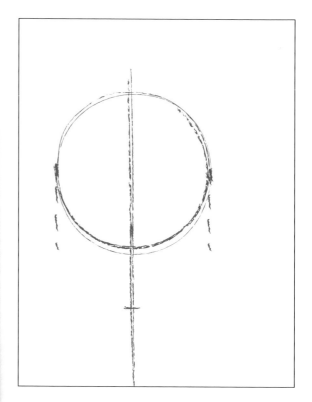

❸ Identify the left and right sides of the circle at the center, its widest point. Draw a mark at each side. Pick one side and lightly pencil in a vertical line from the side of the circle to be level with the bottom of the *circle* (*not* the chin marker that you just drew!). Repeat on the other side. These are guidelines for the jaw.

tip *The placement of the chin marker is going to matter, because it helps keep the correct proportions. Very often, when someone's drawing isn't coming out as they would like, the problem is that they made this mark too high or too far down.*

tip *In my drawing, I show these as dashed lines, so they stand out, but you can lightly draw a solid line. These are simply guidelines that represent the jaw, which will help you get the face right.*

4 Go back to the sides of the circle now, and with those vertical jaw guidelines in place, try making a fluid stroke that gently follows the guideline toward the bottom of the line but then starts to curve toward the chin mark. It's okay if you don't follow the line all the way to the end. This should create a nice egg shape. Naturally, the line you draw will curve a little more than the straight guidelines do and that's okay— they are only there so you don't start rounding toward the chin too soon, which results in an alien-like face shape!

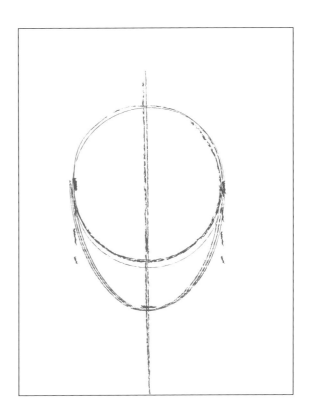

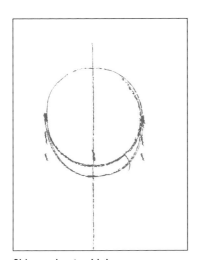

Chin marker too high

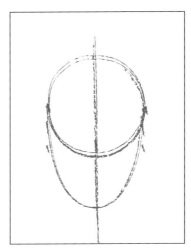

Chin marker too low

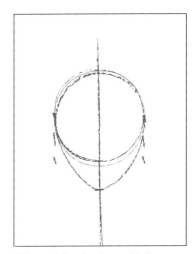

Chin not following jaw guidelines; too pointy

NOTE Of course, the slope and shape of the jaw and chin vary greatly from person to person. This is a *very* general human head shape to get you started, and will help you figure out where other features go.

It's best to start with the face shape as basically an egg shape and then tweak it from there.

Try creating this simple face shape and then draw a modified shape to make up your own.

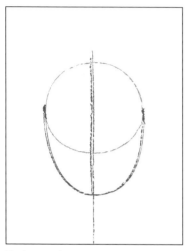

Basic egg shape

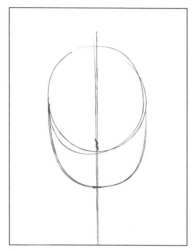

Basic round shape

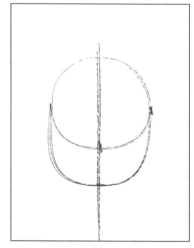

Basic square shape

5 Erase the line noted below.

NOTE: Important! This is very important because it always confuses people—from now on, once you've gotten this far in drawing the face, pretend that the *original circle* we drew at the very beginning doesn't exist. Okay? Never happened. We needed it to build a head, but now, that extra line of the lower half of the circle is just junk that will trip you up. So, erase it— leaving just a lovely, if slightly egg-shaped, head.

Drawing the Neck

❶ Remember that one-third of the circle distance you used to make the chin marker (see Measuring Trick, page 10)? Use that *same dimension* to measure a space below the chin to create the shoulder line. Make a mark at that distance and draw a horizontal line across the page there.

❷ Next make some loose C-curves from slightly below the widest part of the head down to the shoulder line. These don't have to be exact because you are simply putting some rough guidelines in place.

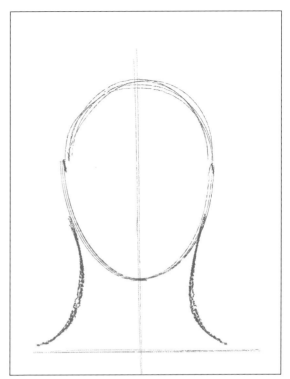

Loose C-curves from just inside sides of head down to shoulder line

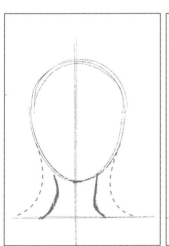

Neck too narrow; bring lines further out toward side of head.

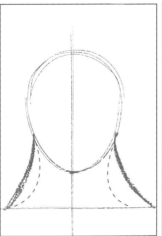

Neck too wide; bring lines in and curve them.

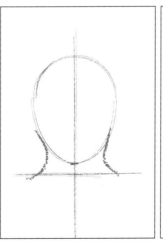

Shoulder line too high; looks like shoulders are hunched up.

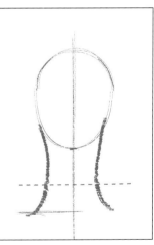

Shoulder line too low; neck too long, raise shoulder line.

CARTOONS

You may notice that the "done wrong" examples (page 13) look kind of cartoony. That's how you make cartoons—you exaggerate different features for comic or stylistic effect. So while they aren't technically *right*, as far as drawing a realistic portrait goes, they aren't completely wrong either. It just depends on what you are trying to achieve. I want to give you a basic understanding of the "proper" locations of features and proportions of the face / head / neck, but you may find that your style is much more cartoonish or stylized and that's not only fine, *it's great*! If it just looks "off," that's one thing and you'll want to work to understand why, but if you're doing it and you like how it looks, then go for it!

Placement of the Features

We'll work on drawing the individual features later, but first you need to know just where to place them on the face. Most of people *think* they know where they go ... until they see what their "before" drawings looks like. Of course, people's features aren't exactly the same shape and size or spaced the same way on the face. These differences are what make us each unique and you will want to notice them, should you choose to do a portrait of a specific person. For our purposes, it's best to start with this general guideline and adjust the placement of features later as you gain confidence and develop your own style.

EYE PLACEMENT

Remember when I said we are going to pretend we never drew that original circle? This is exactly the point where it becomes a problem for people to have that circle still there, so please erase it now if you skipped that step earlier.

1 Identify the top of the head and the *chin marker* (*not* the bottom of the circle that we just erased!), and then make a mark in the center between the 2 markers. Draw a horizontal line across the face at this mark, creating the eyeline. The placement of this line *is* going to matter, so look at the next set of drawings to find where you may need to make an adjustment.

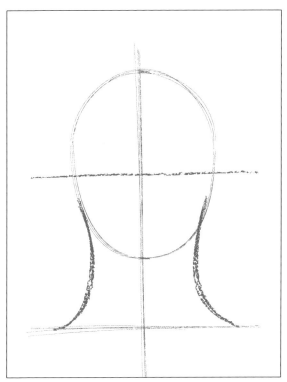

Eyeline halfway between top of head and chin marker

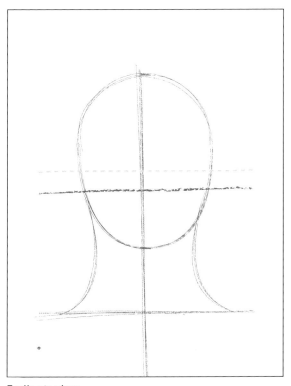

Eyeline too low

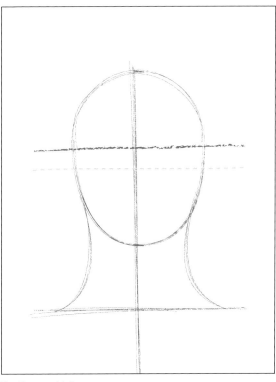

Eyeline too high

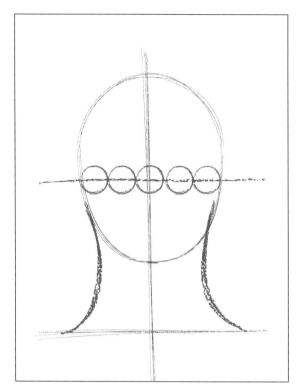

2 A simple trick to get the proportions of the eyes right in relation to the face is to think of the face as 5 eye-widths wide. To create a guide for this, *lightly* pencil in 5 equal-size circles next to each other along the eyeline.

3 Darken the eyeline inside the second and fourth circles to create the eye markers.

---

tip *For extra credit, try drawing a new face with just the two eyeballs roughly where they should be! With practice, you'll be able to place the eyes right where they belong (and in the correct size to fit the face).*

GOING IN CIRCLES?

You may have drawn the circles too large and you don't have enough room to get all five, or too small and you could fit ten! Don't worry, it happens to the best of us!

If you are feeling patient, keep trying until you can draw five circles next to each other that take up the full space between the sides of the head. This kind of "eyeballing" (sorry, not sorry) of the spaces is exactly what you need to learn to be able to draw a face. It takes practice, so try not to expect perfection from yourself. You can approach this problem in two ways.

Option 1

You can either erase and redraw, or, my recommendation is to start a whole new face each time (on a new sheet of paper) using everything you've learned so far so you get more practice with all the other proportions. Drawing these five circles will help you understand roughly the size that the eyes should be in relation to the face. Once you have the five circles drawn, erase the two outer and one center circles, leaving two eyeballs in the correct spots.

Option 2

On the other hand, if you've tried and you just can't do it, here's a shortcut that will give you basically the same result.

Identify the left and right halves of the face, separated by the vertical line in the center. On the eyeline, make a mark in the center of each side. Then, using those marks as a guide, draw two circles *just a little bit* toward the centerline, leaving about an eye-width between them.

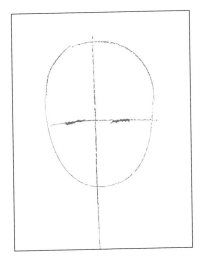
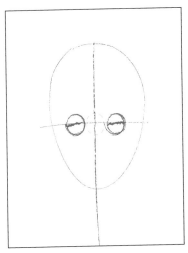

NOSE PLACEMENT

For the placement of the nose marker, first identify the eyeline and the chin marker. Make a small horizontal mark halfway in between them. That's roughly where the bottom of the nose hits.

MOUTH PLACEMENT

For the mouth marker, look at the space between the nose marker and the chin marker. Make a mark roughly a third of that distance down, and make it slightly wider than the nose marker. This line indicates where the space between the lips falls, that dark horizontal line across center of the mouth.

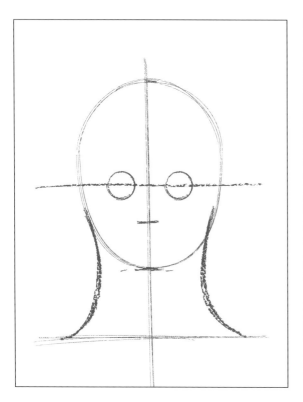

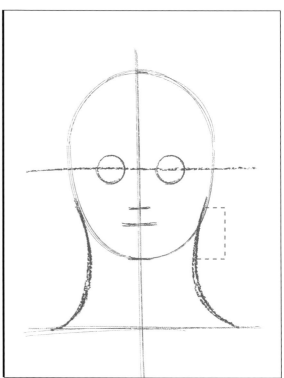

NOTES

- These proportions are not rules—they are guidelines. Some people's lips fall higher or lower on the face and are wider or narrower. You will start to notice these small variations in proportion and placement in your friends' features as you draw more. Ask yourself, "What makes her lips different from mine?"

and see if you can detect all the little differences. It's fun and it will improve your drawing.

- Do you see how this is already looking like a pretty good face, even though it's only some lines representing features? Knowing these markers is a huge step toward being able to draw (and collage) a face.

EYEBROW PLACEMENT

1 Use your fingertips on your own face to identify the location and size of your brows in relation to your eyes. Can you feel how the brows extend beyond the inner and outer corners of the eyes?

2 Draw the eyebrow markers just slightly above the eyeball circles. Make the width of the markers slightly wider than the eye itself. Make sure not to put the eyebrow markers in the middle of the forehead (too high)!

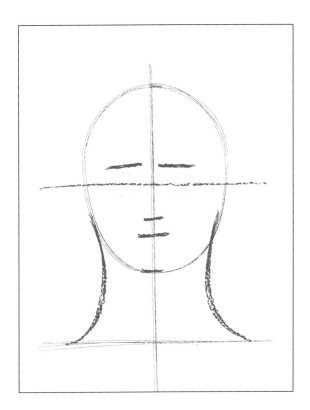

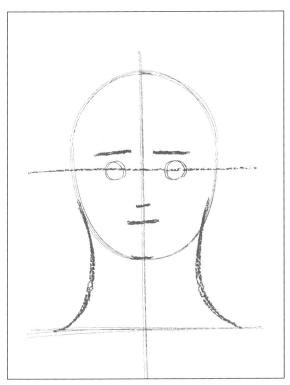

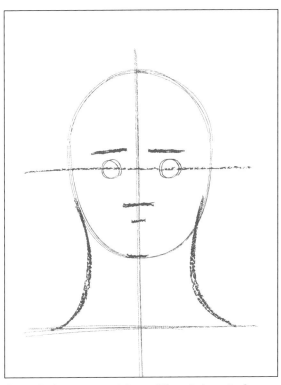

See how just by swapping the width of the nose and mouth markers, the face starts to take on different character? As long as you place them in the correct location, you can make a lot of variations.

EAR PLACEMENT

In class, when we get to this point in the drawing lesson, I ask people to use their own heads as a tool to measure where ears fall in relation to the facial features. I'd like you to do the same.

1 Take your hand to your ear and make a C-shape with your fingers, so your thumb is just touching the bottom of the earlobe and the fingers are gently touching at the top of the ear. Now, holding this width, imagine you could draw a line with the thumb and fingers and slowly "draw" it horizontally toward your face until you meet your eyes.

You have probably found that the fingers come to roughly the center of the eye and the thumb is around the center of the lips. If you can't remember some of the proportions, you always have your own head to use as reference!

2 Draw marks to represent the tops of the ears at the eyeline and draw the bottoms of the ears in line with the mouth marker. Then, draw them into slightly angled rectangles. Remember, this is just a guideline for placement.

Now that you have a well-proportioned guide for drawing the face, all you need to do is learn about the features!

Drawing the Features

In this section, you'll practice drawing each feature on their own, without trying to place them within the face outline. Once you are comfortable drawing the features individually, you can move on to drawing them in position on the face.

Drawing the Eyes

When I teach "Making Faces" as an in-person workshop, easily a third of the drawing lesson is spent on the eyes. You can get most of the proportions and features right, but if the eyes are off, the face won't be that compelling. But if the eyes are right, some other things can be off and it will still look great. As humans, we are innately drawn to look into a being's eyes—our survival requires it! The eyes convey our personality, our light, *our aliveness*—so it's important to spend a little extra time learning about how to portray them.

❶ On a fresh piece of paper, draw a circle (roughly the size of a half-dollar) to represent the eyeball.

NOTE For now, draw the eyes pretty large. Once you move on to placing them on the face, you'll follow the proportions of the face guidelines.

❷ Inside the large circle, draw another circle about half that size. This is the "colory" part of the eye (as I call it in class)—the *iris*. I like to lightly color in the iris with lines that radiate, like the spokes of a wheel. When you move on to fabric you probably won't get that detailed, but it's cool in a drawing.

❸ Within this inner circle, draw another circle about one-third of its size and color it in. That's the *pupil*.

NOTE Since the light or darkness in a room affects the eye, sometimes pupils are a small pinpoint and other times they are almost as large as the iris. For now, draw something in between. Later on, when you want to add personality and variation to your eyes, you can experiment with exaggerating the size of the pupils.

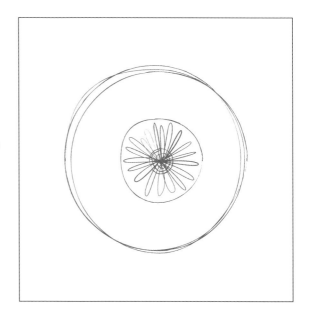

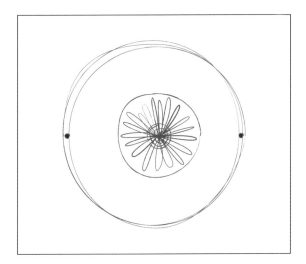 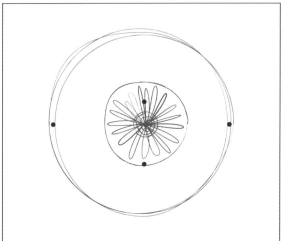

4 Identify the left and the right sides of the eyeball at the widest point and make a little dot in each spot.

5 Mark the bottom of the iris and about half-way between the top of the iris and the pupil. This is going to give you a rough idea of where the lids overlap the eyeball to form the shape of the eye. Most of the time you want the upper lid to be slightly overlapping the iris at the top.

tip *This is just a guideline. Take a look at your eyes in the mirror (or look at photos in magazines) and see if you can notice where the lids fall across the eyeball. Training yourself to notice these subtle details will help you become a better artist.*

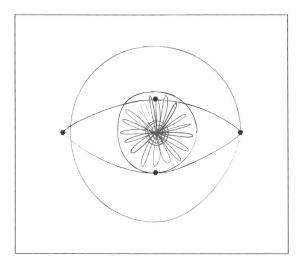

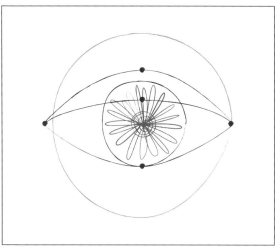

6 Draw a gentle C-curve, connecting the dots from one side of the eye to the other to create the lash line of the upper lid. Repeat for the lower lash line.

7 Mark another dot roughly halfway between the top of the eyeball and the upper lash line (the top line you just drew). Then, draw another C-curve from the outside of the eyeball to connect to that new mark. This creates the line that is crease of the eyelid.

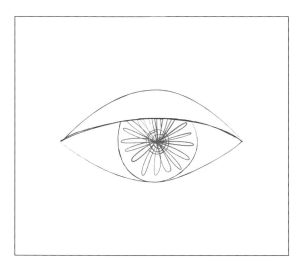

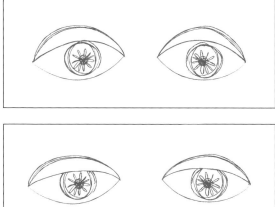

8 Erase the outer eyeball circle and what you are left with is what we think of as an eye! Pretty cool, right?

If the eyes are looking scared (see above, top), adjust the top line of the eye shape so it slightly overlaps the iris (see above, bottom).

NOTE Eventually you won't have to draw all these marks and think about it so much, but it's helpful to have a guideline to go by while you are getting comfortable with the proportions.

PRACTICE MAKES PROGRESS

Now that you have the basic understanding of how to draw an eye, practice drawing them in pairs and varying their shape.

Fold a new sheet of printer paper into four quadrants. Follow Drawing the Eyes, Steps 1–8 (pages 21–23), to draw a new set of eyes in each section.

On each set of eyes, experiment with a different way of drawing the lines that represent the eye opening and the lid crease.

It's okay if the eyes in each set don't match perfectly—most people's eyes don't either.

Thinner lids—less distance between top two lines

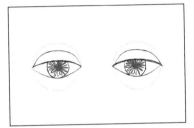

Thicker lids—more distance between top two lines

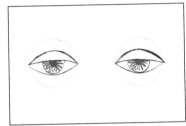

Sleepy lids—lids closer to pupil and more of iris covered

Variations on basic eye instructions

It's fun to experiment with different ways of drawing eyes. Once you know the basics, you can take liberties and create eyes in your own unique way. These stylized eyes all started with the same basic eyeball, iris, and pupil. It's the variation of the lines and curves around that eyeball that makes them look different. Experiment and see what you like.

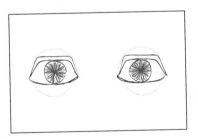

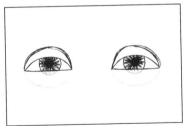

tip *To make the eyes "pop" more, darken the edge of the iris.*

DOT OF LIFE

And now the magical thing that brings the eyes to life: the highlight on the glassy surface of the eyeball, known as the *dot of life*. It's called that because, as you'll see, it really does convey a sense that the eyes are that of a living being.

Look at classic fine art paintings and see if you can detect the white dot that indicates where the light is reflecting off the eye—it's always there. Even cartoons show these highlights! Once you see the dot of life, you'll start to notice it everywhere. Just for fun, see if you can find it in photos or in your own eyes in a mirror.

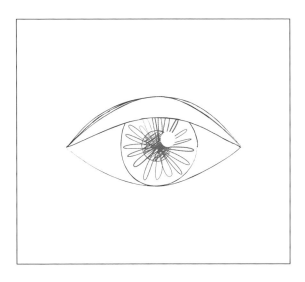

❶ On another sheet, draw an eye in any style you like. The highlight indicates where the light is coming from. To keep it simple, let's have the light source coming from the upper right of the page, which means that the dot of life will be in the upper right of the iris. The highlight should overlap *both* the iris and the pupil.

❷ Use your eraser and remove the pencil marks in a little circle (or a rectangle, wedge shape, crescent, square, or oval) in the upper right of the iris and a little ways into the pupil. It's okay if you remove too much, you can draw it back in after. Draw a light circle around the erased area to define the edge of the highlight and fill in any spots that were erased too much.

If this doesn't show up very well, it may be because the rest of the iris is drawn too lightly to have any contrast. If this is so, color in the iris a bit more and make the pupil the darkest thing. If you like, experiment with making the dot of life larger or smaller, just make sure you still have some pupil showing or it will look odd.

Drawing the Eyebrows

The previous instruction on drawing the eyes will go a long way toward creating a face with life and expression, but the eyebrows are the frosting on the cake! You could take the same set of eyes and draw different eyebrows on them and get totally different looks. When you get to the fabric collage, you can make the eyebrows as simple as a rectangle or take what you learn here and make them in different shapes and experiment with placement to create different expressions.

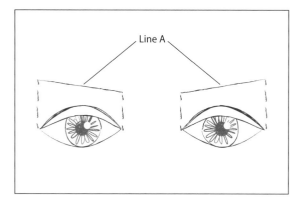

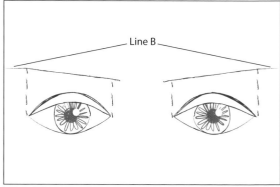

1 At the eyebrow marker, draw line A at a slight angle, directly above and even with the eye. (Refer to Eyebrow Placement, page 19, if needed.) Repeat on other eye.

2 Extend the inside of line A just a little bit beyond on the inner corner of the eye, keeping the same angle. On the outside of line A, draw line B, a short horizontal line that connects to line A. This combination of simple lines creates that classic brow shape. These same eyebrow lines can be filled in or shaped in many different ways.

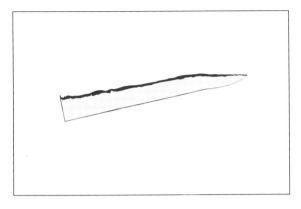

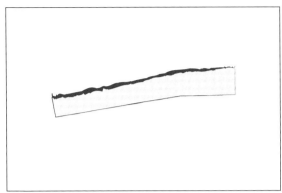

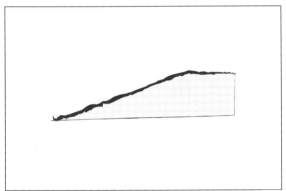

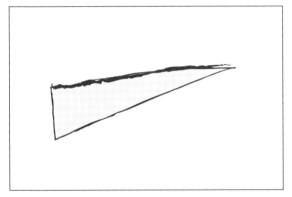

3 On another piece of paper, draw several pairs of eyes and experiment with different angle lines and curves for the brows and different ways of "filling in" the same basic lines. Don't worry too much about drawing brows perfectly. Once we get to the fabric it will be less delicate and more loose and expressive. This is just to give you the idea of how brows are generally shaped.

tip *To understand the variations in eyebrows, look at a lot of photos of different people—or observe people in real life, if you don't mind getting funny looks.*

Of course, eyes also have eye*lashes*, but we won't get into that here. In my collage work I just use a tiny snip of fabric to represent them—a little bit goes a long way.

Drawing the Nose

The nose is more challenging to capture (and teach) than the other features, because it lacks the defined shapes and colors of the eyes and mouth like where the white of the eyeball or the lip color meets the skin. Since the nose is all one color, the variations of highlights and shadows are what gives it shape.

SIMPLE NOSES

Even though I have been drawing and painting faces all my life, I still usually opt for a simple stylized nose, which is what I recommend to my students. Just use one of these lines created from letter shapes and experiment with it until you create your own style.

The L

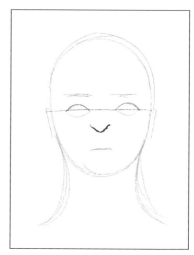
The V

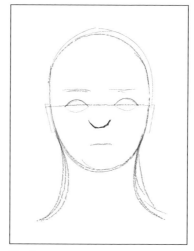
The U

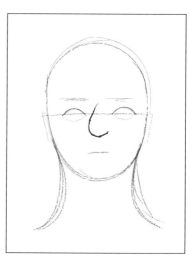
The backward J

"REALISTIC" NOSES

If you want give more realistic noses a try, here is a trick I learned in high school art class.

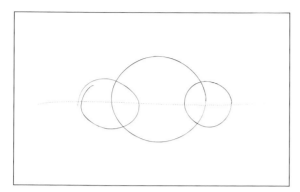 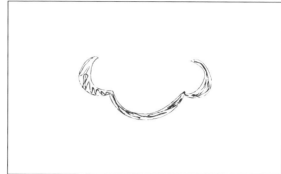

1 Very lightly, draw a horizontal line and then a circle about the size of a nickel centered on it. This represents the main "ball" of the nose. Then, draw (lightly again) a smaller circle on each side, so they overlap the center circle slightly. These represent the sides of the lower portion of the nose, the part that forms around the nostrils.

2 Erase all the lines except the outer side of each smaller circle and the bottoms of all three circles. What you will be left with is a decent looking outline of a nose. This simple line will go a long way toward making a few pieces of fabric look like a nose later on!

Smaller circles above line and not overlapping

Smaller circles below line and not overlapping

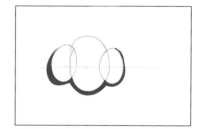

Ovals instead of circles

Using that same trick, you can change the size of the circles and the relationship up or down and it will give you many different variations on a nose. You can also try ovals instead of circles, or whatever you like! Smaller circles of course will make the nose smaller and larger circles will make the nose broader. The placement of this nose up or down on the face in the correct general area will give you more options as well.

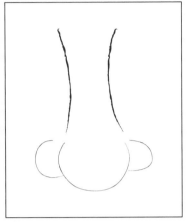 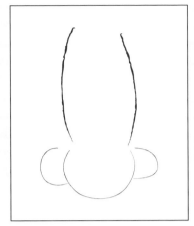 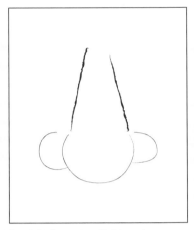

Lines slightly curved inward   **Lines slightly curved outward**   **Straight lines at a slight angle**

You can keep your nose as simple as the line you just learned, or add on to it. Try drawing 1 or 2 lines coming from the brow down toward the sides of the center circle (not to the outer smaller circles). These lines indicate the shadows alongside of the nose. Eventually these will be in fabric or thread, but learning where to place them now is a good foundation, so you don't feel lost when you get to the fabric collage. Try drawing a bunch of different noses and make sure to vary the lines to see how it changes the look.

At the most basic, a nose has the bone/cartilage, the tip, and the nostrils—the rest is just details. Once you understand the general idea, experiment until you create a nose that is unique to your own style. And don't worry too much about realism or perfection!

Drawing the Mouth

The mouth moves and creates a lot of different expressions. Students are usually intimidated by the thought of drawing a face, so I like to set them up for success by keeping it simple. The following instructions focus on drawing the mouth in a neutral, closed position.

Draw a straight line in the center with curved lines on the top and bottom. The line in the center is the shadow of where the mouth opens and closes.

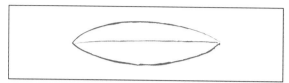

Start with a very basic mouth.

VARIATIONS

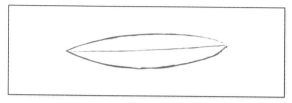

Widen or narrow lips.

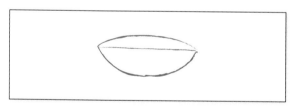
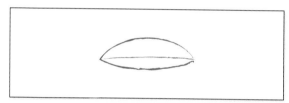

Make one lip thicker than the other.

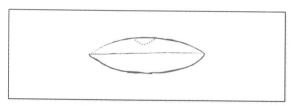
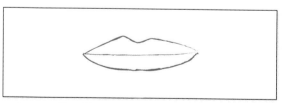

To make lips look more realistic, add some shape to upper lip with a little indent in center.

Draw mouth with top lip wider than bottom lip and vice versa.
Even a small difference between lip widths will change how mouth looks.

tip *Take a look at yourself in a mirror, or look at a friend, or a magazine and see if you can notice the shape of that little notch in the upper lip. Some people barely have one, others have a very pronounced indent.*

  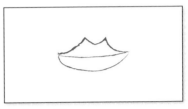

**Even something as simple as varying outer lines on upper lip makes a huge difference.
Straight, curved-out, or curved-in lines create different effects.**

 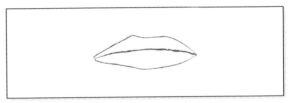

**When you are drawing centerline, slightly curve it up or down and then add upper and lower lip lines.
A slight upturn or downturn of lips makes quite a difference in the mood of the face!**

These are all elements of the mouth you can mix and match to create a great variety of mouths. Additionally, the placing the mouth slightly up or slightly down from the basic mouth marker will vary the look of the face.

Drawing the Hair

In your "before" drawing you may have drawn the hair on the very tip top of the head, standing on end like spaghetti—much like a child's drawing. This is totally normal for a beginner!

There are so many different kinds of hairlines, hair textures, and hairstyles, that it would be impossible to cover them all. What follows is a simple way of defining the hair "shape," which you can then make as detailed as you like with fabric.

The *inside lines* of the hair and the *outside lines* of the hair combine to create the shape of the hair. The inside line of the hair isn't necessarily the real hairline (where the hair starts to grow near the face), although that may indeed be the case. The inside line is where any of the hair meets the face, such as bangs against the forehead or waves against the cheek. To visualize the outside lines, it helps to imagine a photograph of a person in silhouette. The outer edge of the hair silhouette would be the outside line of the hair.

Look at the following examples and notice how the combination of the inside lines (depicted with a solid line) and the outside lines (dashed line) combine to make the shaded *shape of the hair*.

Bangs and hair flowing into neck creates inside lines, and layered style creates spiky outside lines.

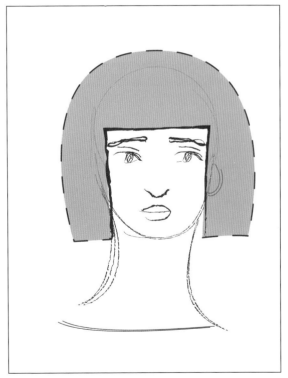

Blunt-cut bangs and hair falling straight at sides creates a dramatic and angular inside line. The outside line basically follows head shape until it reaches sides where hair hangs straight down.

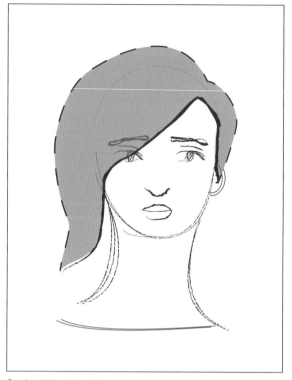

This hairline creates the entire inside line of the hair. You'll usually see this on someone with very short hair or with hair pulled back off the face. The topknot creates an interesting outside line at top of head, and the rest of outside line follows curve of the head.

On the right side of face, hairline *is* the inside line, but the long side-swept bangs drape across left side of face and create the rest of the inside line. The outside line on the right follows the natural shape of the head, but the style and length of hair as it gets longer on the left finish the outside line.

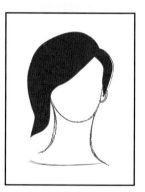

Combined inside lines and outside lines create shape of hair. With features removed, it's easy to see shapes.

"After" Drawing

Now do your "after" drawing! There's no time limit like there was for the "before" drawing. Just grab a new sheet of paper and spend a little time drawing a face informed by your freshly learned knowledge! Keep your "before" and "after" drawings together, so you can see how just a little bit of study goes a long way!

Here are some of my students' "before" and "after" comparisons. That's the difference from the first few minutes of the class until the end, just six hours later. I'll bet yours look just as impressive and they will get even better with more practice and experimentation!

before   after

Angela Garrison

before   after

Elizabeth Furnish

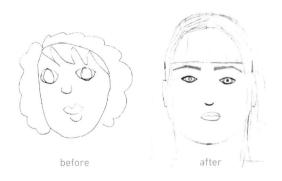

before   after

Tessa Williams

NOTE: Children's Faces You may feel drawn to experiment with drawing and collaging a child's face. Observation, either of a real-life subject or photographs, is the best place to start.

Children's faces have different proportions than adults', especially the eyes in relationship to the rest of the features, head, and face shape, and head *size*, of course! You may also notice children having redder and fuller cheeks, more noticeable eyelashes, and finer eyebrows.

A NOTE ABOUT FACIAL FEATURES

These instructions are meant to help you understand the basic proportions of the human face and give you the confidence to adjust the features to create any face you like. In addition to the range of human skin colors, eyes, noses, and mouths come in a variety of shapes and sizes. Sometimes the differences between our faces are subtle and sometimes they're more obvious. Within these descriptions there are many variations you could portray. As always, observation is key.

Look at photos of the type of feature you want to create (or look in a mirror if you have those features!), and ask yourself the following questions to help you notice what to change about the basic instructions to get the look you're after.

Eyes

How do the inside and outsides of the eyes relate to one another? Is one side more rounded and the other more angular? Are the corners of the eyes on the same plane, or is one side of the eye higher than the other? Is there a visible lid crease? Is the lower lid prominent? Is the eye "hooded," with skin from the brow obscuring part of the eye crease? Are the top and bottom of the eye opening the same, or is one of them more flat or round? Is the upper lid the same thickness across, or does it dramatically taper? Are the eyes closer together or farther apart than the basic proportions? Are the eyebrows fine or bold? What angles create their shape? Do the brows come to a point at the end or are they rounded?

Noses

Is the nose wide or narrow? Is it prominent or shallow? Are the nostrils visible from the front? If so, what shape are they? Does the bottom center of the nose dip down below the nostrils, or is it higher? Are the outsides of the nostrils thick or thin? Does the nose have obvious rounded sections, or is it very subtle? Does it have a bend or crease?

Mouths

Are the lips narrow or wide? Thin or thick? Is one lip thicker or wider than the other? Are the lines of the lips straight, curved, or squarish where they meet the skin? Is there a notch at the top of the upper lip? If so, what shape is it, and is it deep or shallow? Is there a bulb at the bottom of the upper lip? If so, how does that change the center lip line shadow? Do the lips turn slightly up or down at the sides? Are the lips very full, and if so, do they create stronger shadows and highlights?

Asking yourself these questions will help you distinguish the differences in features so you can portray any face you choose.

Chapter Two
Collage

In Chapter One: Draw (page 7), you gained valuable knowledge about the proportions and features of the face. Now you get to put that into practice using fabric, scissors, and glue!

In this chapter, you'll find all the information I share with students who take my workshops. I offer advice on which fabrics and adhesives to use, how to create facial features in fabric, and all my best tips and tricks.

Fabric

I generally use 100% cotton quilting fabric; there are so many awesome colors and prints to choose from. The following suggestions refer to quilting cotton, but you can certainly use other fabrics.

Obviously color is going to play a major role in your collage, but first let's talk about solids versus printed fabrics.

Solids

The simplest choice is to use solid-color fabric. You don't have to worry about whether the design is too big or has too much contrast—it's one simple color. Solids work well for both base fabrics and features.

BASE FABRICS

When following the basic instructions, the base fabric *is* the skin color, but it doesn't have to stay that way. You can layer many similar colored fabrics all over the face to create variations and totally change or add to texture to the skin.

When selecting fabrics to use as the base of the collage, keep in mind that you want the features to stand out on whatever you choose. Solids and very subtle prints are ideal.

While it may seem like you should start with a white piece of fabric—like starting a drawing on a plain white sheet of paper— I have found that white fabric does *not* make the best base fabric for this technique. For beginners, it's best to choose a base fabric that will contrast at least a little bit with the white eye shape that is one of the first elements we put down. To see if your base fabric choice is too light, cut a small piece of white fabric and lay it on top. If the white doesn't stand out at least a little, try a darker fabric.

Prints

Not all prints work great for making faces. I think the eyes should be the most compelling part of the face, so I counsel students to stay away from prints that will distract from that important feature. Here are some examples of which fabrics to use liberally and those to avoid.

BEST PRINTS TO USE

You want the features you've created be the star of the show, so it's important to choose fabrics that don't compete with them. *Tonal* designs, also referred to as *tone-on-tone* or *two-tone*, are those that are two shades of the same color—such as medium blue with a slightly darker blue print or black with a very dark gray print. They are generally subtle and have low contrast. These and small-scale prints with low contrast are ideal for facial features because they lend texture and variation in color. If you squint your eyes, these prints almost read as a solid and add variation without being overwhelming. Gather a variety of these to use with your solids and you'll have all the fabric you need to make some awesome faces.

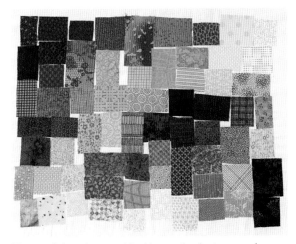

These subtle prints are ideal to use for features and backgrounds.

PRINTS TO USE CAREFULLY

Large prints and busy small prints—those with a lot of contrast—can be difficult to use. If the design is too big it may confuse the eye once it's cut up into a small piece and used in a facial feature. These kinds of challenging prints are best used once you gain experience or want to break some rules.

Large-scale and high-contrast prints will compete with features you create, so use them sparingly.

USING NONQUILTING FABRICS

After you've made a few faces, you might like to experiment with different types of fabric to see if any call your name. Think about how cool that lace would look as skin! What about metallic dancewear fabric as jewelry? Or burlap hair? Great things happen when you keep an open mind and a playful attitude. As long as your sewing machine can get through it, you're good!

USING FABRIC MOTIFS AS DESIGN ELEMENTS

While I do recommend staying away from large prints for the features, you can still incorporate a beloved busy fabric into your artwork. You may find that your precious swatch will work perfectly in the hair, whether fussy cut as whimsical cheeks or as part of the background.

Once you start making faces, you'll probably find that you look at familiar fabrics in a whole new light. You may look at a floral print and think the center of a flower would make the perfect iris. Maybe you find a print with circles containing geometric patterns and you say to yourself, *Cheeks!* or *That foliage print has leaves that are the perfect lip shape!* or *This swirly fabric would make perfect wavy hair!* or *Ooh, I'll cut out this bird and have it perched on my lady's shoulder or build a nest in her hair!*

Yes! Go with your weird ideas—this is how you develop your own style!

Color Choices

How you use color will have a huge impact on the look of your faces. Some people prefer a realistic approach, approximating skin tones and hair colors and even trying to make the features look like a specific person's. Others opt to take a more playful point of view.

I have the most fun when I toss out preconceived ideas of what skin color or a particular nose looks like and just let my imagination lead me. While I do always use white fabric (or very light) for the whites of the eyes and black (or very dark) for the pupils, everything else is fair game! I encourage you to experiment with both realistic coloring and more expressive and even wacky coloring.

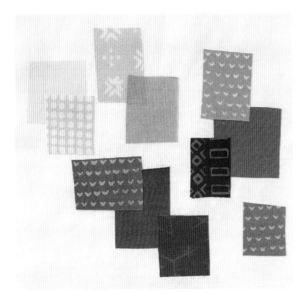

Creating a face with a realistic palette can be hard to get right, but it is appealing to many beginners because they want it to look like a "real face."

A not-so-realistic palette is more forgiving and a lot more fun.

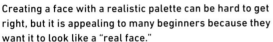

tip *Try making a face completely with one type of fabric—striped fabrics, shot cotton, or batiks. It might seem counterintuitive, but sometimes limiting your choices enhances your creativity.*

LET'S TALK ABOUT VALUE

There's a saying I like: "Color gets the credit, but value does the work." This means it's not necessarily the *color* (orange, for example) that is making something look great, but the *value* of that color (the lightness or darkness of it) that makes the difference. A darker orange might create a great contrast with what is next to it, whereas a lighter orange might not. It's the interest achieved by using different values that makes a work compelling to look at.

As an extreme example, imagine making a face in all different values of orange. You could have very dark, almost black-orange and a very light, almost white-orange and everything in between. You'd be able to create a great looking image with that palette, even though they are all "orange."

But imagine if I gave you a stack of orange fabrics that, though they may be different prints, all read as the same value of orange—a medium-value orange. There would be no way to make the eyes stand out or add definition to the lips, right?

That's a simple way to explain importance of value, but the real understanding comes from the experience you gain each time you try different colors or values in your own work.

Supplies

Before you start rummaging through your supplies, let me tell you a little about the stuff I like to use.

Adhesives

Since the small pieces of fabric need to be held in place until the collage can be stitched down, you'll need something to stick them down.

WASHABLE GLUE STICK

For the larger pieces or for first positioning, I use an Elmer's Washable Glue Stick. Since I like to be able to reposition pieces as I go, I don't want to glue them firmly in place until I'm ready to stitch them down. A quick swipe with a glue stick works perfectly for this.

LIQUID GLUE WITH AN EXTRAFINE GLUE TIP

Once you have lightly tacked all the bits down with a glue stick, it's time to glue down the edges of the fabrics to make sure they don't flip up as you stitch them down. For this step, I like Elmer's Washable School Glue, the white stuff you can find everywhere. In some cases, you may opt to use permanent fabric glue (such as Liquid Stitch Permanent Adhesive by Dritz). For tips on choosing a glue type, see Should I Use Washable or Permanent Glue? (next page).

One of my favorite products is an extrafine glue tip (such as Micro Fine Glue Tips by Sharon Schamber) that screws right onto standard-size glue bottles. The tip is *so fine* that it can take a while to squeeze the glue through it! As I'm working, I often lay the bottle on its side, so the glue is already halfway there. Sometimes I even clip off a tiny bit of the tip, to make the hole ever-so-slightly bigger. The stream of glue is still very fine even when you widen the opening a bit.

If you don't have access to one of the fine glue tips, you can always use the tip that comes with the glue. Make sure to open the tip only enough to let *some* glue come out, not the full stream, since you are going to be stitching the fabric down and the glue is just to hold it in place until you do. Using the original tip this way is not as elegant as using the special fine tip, but it does the job.

Assortment of supplies

SHOULD I USE WASHABLE OR PERMANENT GLUE?

My first answer is usually, "Use whatever you already have!" But sometimes there are reasons other than convenience for choosing one over the other.

If you know you are going to stitch all your fabrics quite a lot, appreciate the rawness of raw-edge appliqué, or are making a wallhanging, then I say use the washable glue you probably already have on hand.

If you know your project will get a lot of wear (a garment, quilt, or bag), may be laundered, or you just prefer to minimize the rawness of your edges, you may opt to use a permanent fabric

glue like Liquid Stitch Permanent Adhesive instead of the washable glue. In the event that you neglect to stitch down a couple corners, washable school glue will, of course, *wash out*. In that case, you run the risk of that flap of fabric getting caught and pulling out stitches, which may result in losing some detail pieces. Permanent fabric glue will keep them adhered to the base fabric and, if glued right up to the edges, will cut down on fraying. In the case of a wallhanging, this won't matter, because it will be handled infrequently and is unlikely to be washed.

FUSIBLE WEB

Although I almost always use a glue stick to tack down the pieces, followed by liquid glue with a fine glue tip to secure the edges of my fabrics, sometimes using lightweight fusible web (such as Heat*n*Bond Lite or Mistyfuse) is the right choice. Fusible web is a magical iron-on adhesive that usually comes in paper-backed sheets. It really only makes sense to use it if you can start with larger pieces of fabric of at least 4″ × 4″ (rather than scraps), because it would be tedious to apply fusible web to the back of odd-shaped or small pieces of fabric. You can still cut small shapes out of the treated fabric, but you wouldn't want to start with small pieces and then add the web.

Apply the fusible (as it's often referred to) on the wrong side of the fabric, according to the manufacturer's instructions. If it has paper, remove it and you will be left with a piece of fabric that has a shiny coat of adhesive on the back. Cut small pieces from this fabric and place them shiny side down on your collage. Consult the instructions for the brand of fusible that you have and use an iron to melt the adhesive in place.

BENEFITS AND DRAWBACKS OF USING FUSIBLE WEB

Benefits

- It creates a very secure bond.

- It minimizes raw edges.

- You can cut tiny detail pieces that won't fall apart.

Drawbacks

- It's not repositionable.

- The layer of adhesive adds a little stiffness to the piece. (If this is a concern, use Mistyfuse because it has a reputation for being the finest fusible, allowing for more drape than others.)

- Best used with larger pieces of fabric instead of scraps.

- Once the adhesive is on the back of your fabric, you've committed to using the fabric in that way because the adhesive can't be removed.

Tools

Scissors

Use sharp fabric scissors, just as you would for any project where you are cutting fabric freehand (as opposed to using a rotary cutter) and it's good to have a set of small embroidery scissors on hand as well. While it makes sense to use small scissors on the tiny details like pupils and the dot of life, I prefer to use regular-size fabric scissors most of the time. I find it helps to keep my approach loose and free. If you find you are using the small scissors a lot and getting too detailed and perfection-oriented on things other than the tiniest details, try switching to regular fabric scissors and cut larger pieces of fabric.

Tweezers

Some people like to use tweezers to place small fabric pieces on their collage. As with the tiny embroidery scissors, using tweezers tends to encourage you to use tiny pieces—sometimes to your detriment! There's nothing wrong with detailed work, but it can lead to a perfectionist attitude and unhelpful fussing. Of course, sometimes it is just easier to use a tool to place something, so go ahead and use tweezers, if you like.

tip I don't usually have tweezers on hand, so I use a pin to stab the tiny piece, put a dab of glue on it, and place it on the collage.

USE YOUR PHONE CAMERA

While not on the supply list, having a smartphone for taking quick photos is a valuable tool. I always use mine for this purpose and encourage students to take photos of their work in class. It's not only a lot of fun to look at the progression of a face from just a few scraps to a full collage, but it helps shape the work, as well. Sometimes seeing your collage reduced onto a phone screen helps you see things that you want to add or remove.

You can further evaluate the image by putting a black-and-white filter on the picture. This allows you to remove color from the equation and see only the value contrast in your face (see Let's Talk about Value, page 41). By looking at your work this way, you may realize you have too many mid-tones and not enough contrasting lights and darks.

It's always a good idea to step back and assess your work, and using photos is one of my favorite ways to do this.

If you do take pictures of your work, please share them with me on social media (see About the Author, page 111). I'd love to see what you create!

Make the Collage

Follow these basic steps to create the features. If you need to review proportion and shaping features, refer back to Chapter One: Draw (page 7). Once you get the basics down, you can start to add more personality and depth by incorporating the information from the Next Level sidebars for each feature.

OUTLINE, ROUGH DRAFT, FINAL EDIT

When you're writing a story, you make notes and write a rough draft first. It doesn't come out well written and perfect the first time, right? You edit and finesse the draft until it takes shape. Making visual art is the same. You get started, put some stuff down, and then figure out how to make it better. Fixing, changing, or removing parts you don't like is part of the process.

Think of completing the basic instructions as writing an outline. Once you have these down, you can go back and create the rough draft by looking at the Next Level sidebars. That's where you'll find those extra tips and ideas for each feature that will help you add more depth and personality to your work.

When it comes to editing and polishing the final collage, assessment is key. For some questions to ask yourself that will help you see where you might need to make some changes, see Assess Your Work (page 53).

Add Markers of the Face to the Base Fabric

Start with a roughly fat quarter–size piece of the base fabric (see Base Fabrics, page 38).

NOTE Quilting cottons are often sold in units called *fat quarters*. It is a quarter yard of fabric that, instead of being long and skinny as if cut off a bolt of fabric, is a project-friendly rectangular piece measuring roughly 18″ × 22″.

In Chapter One: Draw (page 7), you practiced creating a head shape. Now, when we're creating the collage with fabric pieces, we are going to forego making a head shape in favor of simply marking the top of the head and the chin. The head shape is formed mainly by the hair shape and jawline, which will be added later.

Cut small pieces of a contrasting fabric to use as the top of the head and chin markers, as well as the markers of the face—eyes, nose, and mouth. Lay these on the base fabric to act as placeholders for the features, referring back to Chapter One for proportions, if necessary. Do *not* glue these down.

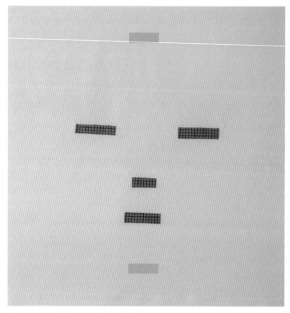

Markers of face on base fabric

tip *If you prefer, you can use tailor's chalk to mark the base fabric instead of using fabric.*

VARYING PROPORTIONS

Once the markers are placed in the "right" spots, play with subtle changes that express your own preferences and taste. Try moving one feature at a time just slightly to see if you'd like to use a stylized set of proportions, such as wider-set and lowered eyes. You could also try increasing or decreasing the width of the markers; for example, making a much narrower mouth or wider nose. Over time, you will gain confidence in your choices and develop your signature style.

Step Away from the Project

Once I get going on a creative project, it can be hours before I get up from my work. While it feels awesome to be so focused and inspired, there is a huge benefit to getting up and looking at the piece from a different perspective. Very often when I look at it from a vantage point of something other than a few inches away, I find that something I was struggling with or wasn't sure about actually looks great.

And sometimes *it doesn't*, which is another good reason to walk away for a bit! Continuing to work on something that isn't coming together can be frustrating and counterproductive. If you are getting hung up on a feature or detail, move along and come back to it later.

Eyes

1 Cut shapes for the whites of the eyes and replace the eye markers with them, spaced roughly one eye-width apart. If you like the size and placement, tack them down with the glue stick.

tip *Don't bother trying to smear the glue stick over the entire back of the fabric or getting right up to the edges. In this "tacking down" stage, simply give the back of the fabric a quick swipe with the glue stick—just enough to hold it in place until you get to the finer gluing later.*

2 Cut out the iris and tack in place on the white eye shape.

tip *Make sure the iris color will contrast with the black of the pupil. A medium brown iris will look better than a very dark brown iris because the contrast between the pupil and the iris help to make the eye really pop.*

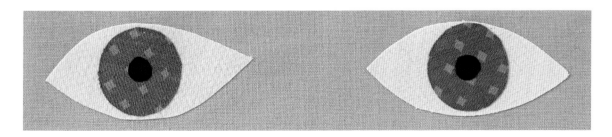

3 Cut out black fabric circles for the pupils and tack down in the center of the iris—make them small enough so the iris color still shows, but not so small that the dot of life (page 25) will completely cover them.

EYELIDS

The eyelids should be as wide as the eye shape and generally follow the same curve as the top of the eye shape. If you are using an almond shape for the white of the eye, your eyelid shape will be a crescent.

Use a fabric that is either slightly darker or lighter than the base fabric. If you use a fabric that is too similar to the base fabric, the lids will not show up well.

Cut 2 eyelid shapes. Lay the eyelid piece at the top of the eye shape, so it is slightly overlapping the iris and glue in place. If the lids don't partially overlap the top of the iris, the eyes will have a surprised or scared expression.

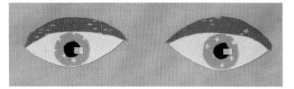

Surprised or scared

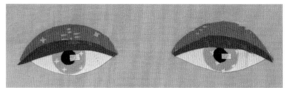

Add another thin crescent to change the surprised look.

FINISHING THE EYES

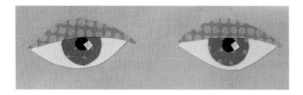

❶ Cut 2 dots of life (page 25) from white fabric and glue in place according to the direction of your chosen light source (see Dot of Life, Step 1, page 25). Remember this piece should slightly overlap *both* the iris and the pupil. Notice how the eyes come alive with just that one little detail!

❷ Cut 2 eyebrows. Experiment with slight adjustments to the placement if desired and tack down. Keep in mind that eyebrows can be as simple as rectangles and you can change them as the face develops.

---

tip *If you labor over cutting out the pieces, try letting go a little and see if you can make some imperfect and quick cuts. You may enjoy the process more if you can allow yourself to be expressive and free rather than tight and controlled.*

NEXT LEVEL: EYES

The eyes are my favorite part! Here are some tips for taking them beyond the basics.

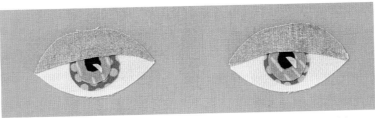

Layer a second, smaller circle on iris in a shade slightly different from iris. Make this circle large enough that it will still show once you add pupil.

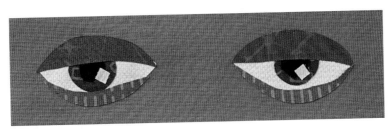

Add thinner lower lid.

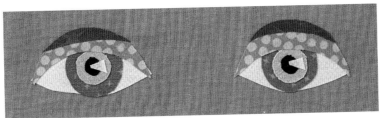

In darker fabric than lid color, add a second thinner lid layer along top of lid to indicate the crease of the eyelid. This can be the full width of the lid or just a little crescent.

Add a very dark, thin strip along lash line (where eye and lid meet) to indicate eyelashes. This line can extend a little beyond outside of eye.

Nose

As you gain experience you will naturally develop your own way of making noses, but to start, keep it simple.

Look at the examples of noses in Chapter One: Draw (see Drawing the Nose, page 28). Cut the simple shapes to create the nose you like. Remove the nose marker and experiment with nose placement, if desired. Tack it in place.

NEXT LEVEL: NOSES

I can't stress enough that the nose can be very simple and still look great, but if you want to experiment, have at it! For more ideas, refer to "Realistic" Noses (page 29). Use fabric that is slightly darker than the base fabric for the following tips.

• Add crescent shapes to indicate shadows along the outer edges of the nose around the nostrils.

• Use a snip of fabric to create a shadow under the bottom of the nose.

• Add crescent shapes at the inner edges of the eyebrows to indicate the bridge of the nose.

• With a darker fabric, experiment with cutting flattened ovals to indicate the shadows of the nostril.

NOTE "Learn the rules like a pro, so you can break them like an artist."

This quote is often attributed to Pablo Picasso, but is not verified. Whether he's the one who said it or not, it's a great quote!

Mouth

As with all the features, you can create an effective mouth with just a few snips of fabric.

Keeping in mind that lip colors should show up on the base fabric, cut out the lip shapes, using a slightly darker fabric for the upper lip. Remove the mouth marker and replace it with lip shapes, adjusting placement, if desired. Tack down. Cut a thin strip of a dark fabric (darker than the lips) and glue in place between the lips.

tip *Remember to take process photos!*

NEXT LEVEL: MOUTHS

I gave this tip in the basic instructions, but it bears repeating: Make the upper lip slightly darker than the lower lip. This will instantly add dimension to the mouth.

- Add a highlight in the center of the lower lip by cutting a jelly-bean shape from fabric that is just slightly lighter than the color of the lower lip.

- Create a shadow under the lower lip by adding a thin strip of fabric that is slightly darker than the base color.

- If desired, experiment with adding smile lines at the outer corners of the mouth by cutting thin snips of fabric in a slightly lighter or slightly darker color than the base fabric. It's easy to overdo it, so step back and assess before you commit to it.

- Use a subtle snip of fabric to indicate the indent between the mouth and the nose.

Choose a fabric that is *only very slightly* darker than the base fabric to avoid having it look like a moustache.

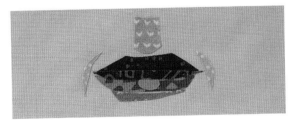

Shadow under lower lip, slight smile lines, and indent between nose and mouth

Chin

Cut a thin strip of fabric and glue in place of the chin marker.

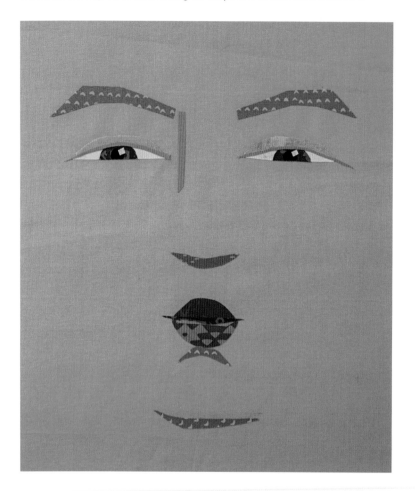

CHIN IDEAS

While the chin isn't quite as compelling as the lips or eyes, there are a few more things you could do to add more interest to this area. For all these tips, use a fabric that is slightly darker than the base fabric.

• Indicate the "ball" of the chin—that semicircle shaped crease a little below the mouth—by adding a crescent moon shape.

• Create a dimple with a small snip of fabric placed near the bottom of the chin. Avoid making dimples too dark or you risk them looking like moles rather than shadows.

• Add a shadow under the chin line with another crescent shape.

Assess Your Work

As the collage starts to develop, here are some questions to help you do some fine-tuning and correct anything that may be off.

The first thing to assess is whether the features are in proportion (in the right spots in relation to each other). Are the eyebrows placed way up where the hairline will be (too high)? Is the mouth in the middle of the chin (too low)? If you need a refresher, refer to It's All about the Proportions (page 9). Correct any proportion issues and move on.

Next, go feature by feature and ask yourself if you like each one and correct what you don't like. If you get stuck on something, try to break it down to figure out what you don't like about it. For example, with the eyes: Do you want to try them closer together or farther apart? Are they placed too high on the face? Do you like the lid shape? Did you remember the dot of life? Is there enough contrast between the iris and the pupil or the white of the eye and the base fabric? Is the fabric used in the brows too busy?

After you review all the features, look at the face overall. Do you want to add more color? Is there enough contrast to make the features stand out? Is the face too busy or too plain?

Don't worry if you have a lot of adjustments to make. It takes some time and practice to learn how to draw a face and then create it in fabric. Be patient with yourself and enjoy the process.

Hair

Create the hair using thin strips of fabric to act as the inside and outside lines of the hair (refer to Drawing the Hair, page 33). Fill in as desired and tack down.

Or you can experiment with cutting elongated almond shapes in different sizes and layering them to create the hair shape. You could add snips of other colors to create more depth once you have the basic shape filled in.

- *To help you visualize the hair shape, try draping a long piece of yarn around the collaged face to act as the inside and outside lines of the hair.*

- *Don't try to cut the hair shape all in one piece of fabric. It looks best when you use multiple pieces to build up the shape. This also keeps it from looking like a hair "helmet"!*

- *Avoid using large swaths of a single solid fabric, unless you plan to put some texture into it with stitching.*

- *Experiment with incorporating both lighter and darker colors with the main hair color to create more depth.*

Ears

Ears, while not exactly considered *optional*, are not always visible. Whether you add them depends on if they would be seen with the hair shape you create. If so, cut semicircles (lobe) or half-ovals (whole ear) and glue in place.

I like to keep the ears simple. They can be as uncomplicated as a semicircle that you put down and then cover partially with hair fabrics. Look around you at people nearby or at photos of people in a magazine. See how in most cases, their ears are not fully showing? Unless we are talking about someone with a very short haircut or with long hair intentionally pushed behind their ears, most people have some hair falling over and obscuring the top part of the ear.

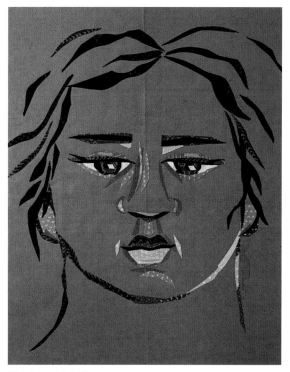

Simple semicircle ears

Going Beyond the Basics

I've given step-by-step instructions for creating the face and Next Level ideas for the basic features to take them even further. Now it's your turn to express your own unique style. Take a look at these examples of different ways I've stylized the same basic elements. Once you know the basics of the features and proportions of the face, you get to bend the rules to create in your own signature style!

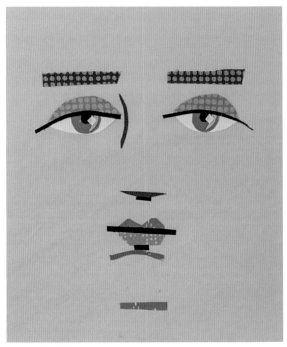

"Drawing" with black fabric "lines" lends an illustrative vibe.

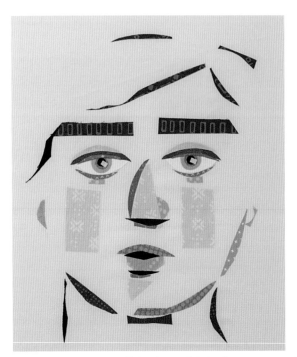

Using larger fabric pieces cut at angles creates an abstract impression.

Completely filling in skin areas with fabric pieces produces that classic art quilt look.

You don't have to stop here! On your next piece, start with a larger base fabric and experiment with adding more fabric to create a background behind your person. This might be different pieces of fabric tacked down to add texture or maybe you want to get more detailed and make a scene or environment for your person.

tip *Believe it or not, looking at your piece upside down can help to solve issues you may have. When the collage is upside down, it's easier to distance yourself from what you are trying to make—a face—and look at it simply as a design made of colors and shapes. This helps you to see where you need to make changes.*

Additional Details

Once you've made it this far, you've created a basic face already. You could make sure the edges of your fabrics are well secured to the base fabric, and then move on to Chapter Three: Stitch (page 61) for stitching information or to incorporate any of the following details that speak to you.

Cheeks

Here are few ways to incorporate cheeks into your collage.

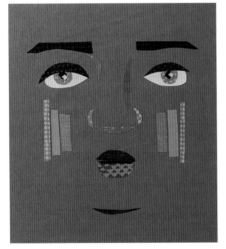

Place strips of similarly colored fabric next to each other.

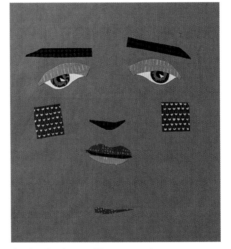

Cut basic shapes like rectangles, squares, or triangles in fabric slightly lighter or darker than base fabric.

tip *Generally we think of these as human features, but you could cut the face out in a circle shape, add rays, and create a sun face. Get creative and use the technique however you like.*

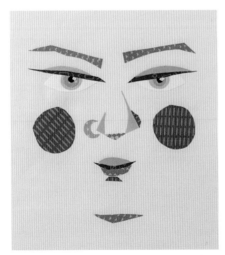

Make stylized, doll-like cheeks from circles of fabric.

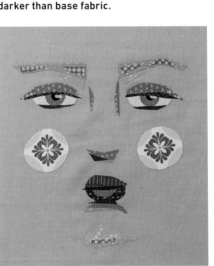

Use a fabric motif for a whimsical look.

Jawline

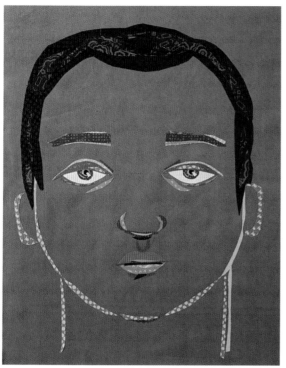

To create jawline, you can cut small snippets of fabric to act as a line that you would draw if you were using pen or paint.

Wrinkles

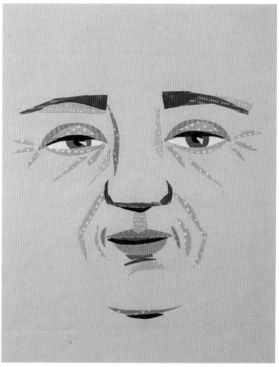

When creating wrinkles, it helps to think of them as "parentheses" around mouth or "whiskers" around outside of eyes. Unless you are intentionally collaging a face that you want to look old, limit wrinkles to just a few lines made with thin snips of fabric just a step darker or lighter than skin tone.

tip *Keep in mind that this might be your first time collaging a face, so be gentle with yourself! They can't all be gems. Sometimes you are going to make something ugly and that's okay. I certainly have made my share of stuff that just didn't work. No big deal.*

Making Men's Faces

I focus on teaching how to make women's faces, but there are a few simple things you can do to tweak my instructions to make a man's face. Simple adjustments can make the face look more masculine. Of course, men have a lot of different looks, but if you are going for the stereotypical masculine-looking man, here are some things to consider.

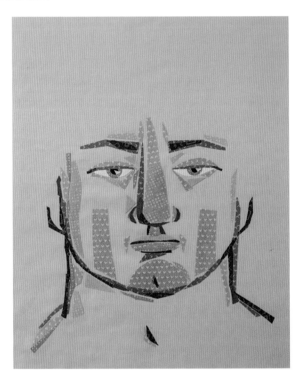

- Broaden the neck and give fuller shoulders (if they're showing).

- Make the features larger to take up a little more room on the face.

- Create wider and thicker brows.

- Use beiges and browns for lips, rather than pinks and reds.

- Consider adding an Adam's apple with a crescent shape of fabric in a shade slightly darker than the skin color.

- Hair style and facial hair will go a long way toward making the face look like a man, just try to keep the facial hair from getting too cartoony! Start with colors just a little darker than the skin tone and build up the darkness.

Gluing Edges

If the collage is large, it can take a few hours to use the fine glue tip to tack down all the edges. Take your time, binge watch some Netflix shows and get it done. The edges may still flip up when sewing, no matter how hard you tried to tack them down with your fine glue tip. Don't fret about it! When you look at the final piece with all the stitching and texture, you'll never notice a couple of turned-up edges!

Chapter Three
Stitch

You've collaged a fabric face and now it's time to finish it by sewing it all down. Stitching secures the fabrics and adds textural interest to your work. In this chapter we'll talk about fabric stabilizers, thread choices, and simple stitching options.

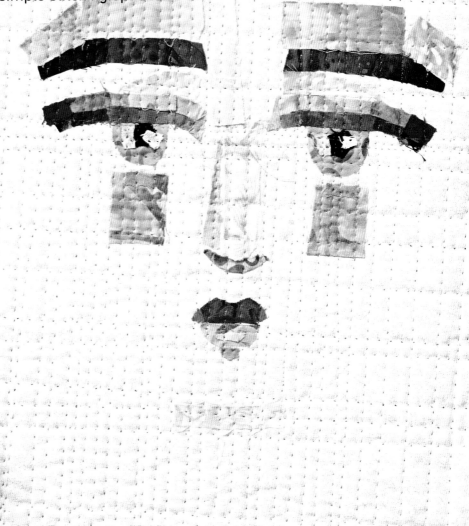

Stabilizers

A stabilizer is used so the fabric doesn't pucker with the application of machine stitching. Here are some examples of what stitched fabric looks like using various stabilizers.

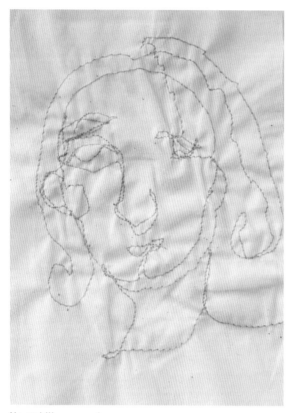

No stabilizer = puckers

Lightweight fusible interfacing, used in garment making

Which Stabilizer Should I Use?

How you intend to use your face panel is what will guide your stabilizer choice. If you are making a pillow, a thicker stabilizer such as a lightweight cotton batting or cotton/poly blend batting would be perfect. Conversely, if you want to use your collage as a front yoke or panel in a dress, I'd suggest a lightweight fusible interfacing, because it will be thinner and maintain more drape than if batting were used. Generally, the thicker or stiffer the stabilizing material, the nicer the stitches look—but you sacrifice softness and the drape of the fabric.

Medium-weight sew-in interfacing, commonly used to stabilize dense machine embroidery

Lightweight cotton/poly blend batting in center, quilting fabric underneath

---

tip *If you have a specific result in mind, test each of the stabilizers to see which one gives you to look you want.*

Thread

As you gain experience with the basic techniques, you can experiment with different thread types and stitching, but to start, it's best to stick with the basics.

All-Purpose Thread

You can't go wrong using all-purpose thread in a color that blends well with most of the collage. A good way to test this is to pull a couple feet of thread off the spool, gather it all in one hand, and drop it on top of the collage. It will spread a bit, but the thread will be concentrated enough that you can get a sense of what it would look like stitched all over the piece. If the thread color seems to disappear into the face, it would be considered a "blending" thread.

Blending thread and contrasting thread

Poly or Nylon Thread

The one other thread I sometimes use is poly (or nylon) invisible thread (with regular all-purpose thread in the bobbin). The various brands behave differently depending on the sewing machine, so you'll need to experiment to find what works best for your setup. I use poly thread when I want to stitch down my collage without adding any color. This is particularly useful if I have created small details that would be obscured by a regular thread.

GIVE POLY A CHANCE

Poly/nylon thread has kind of a bad rap. Whenever I mention it as an option in class, I can feel students cringing at the idea. People still think of it as what used to be stitched on commercially produced comforters in the 80s—a wiry, thick fishing line type of material. But it's totally different now! The manufacturers have improved it over the years—it's finer, more supple, and less shiny. I sometimes use it on full-size bed quilts; I think it looks great, and doesn't feel much different from all-purpose thread. Poly/nylon thread is an excellent choice for all kinds of art quilting, so if you have a bias against it, I urge you to give it another try.

Stitching

Sometimes I hear from a student who worries that stitching over the collage is going to ruin the face. I reassure them that this is akin to thinking that quilting will ruin the look of quilt blocks! It's simply not true! Thread lines add a wonderful new dimension to your collage.

Of course, if you have a light-colored face and you want to do some very close together straight lines of stitching, you'd probably want to use a blending thread color, rather than say, black, right? When in doubt, make a test piece and try out your thread choice.

Free-Motion Stitching

The easiest way to stitch your collage is with *free-motion quilting* (often abbreviated FMQ). This technique allows you to sew in any direction as you feed the fabric under the sewing machine needle. You can free-motion quilt on your domestic machine as long as you can lower the feed dogs. You also need to use a specialty foot meant for this purpose, such as a darning foot, hopping foot, or free-motion foot. These feet hop up and down with the needle, so when the needle is up the fabric can move freely, and when the needle is down, the foot stabilizes the fabric to ensure good stitch quality.

NEVER TRIED FREE-MOTION STITCHING BEFORE?

You've got your feed dogs down and the special foot installed, now it's time to play. Layer some quilt batting between two fat quarters to make a quilt sandwich to practice on.

• Hold the piece flat with both hands to feed it under the needle.

• Keeping your machine speed steady, try moving the fabric at different speeds and notice how this affects the stitch length. If your stitches are really long, slow down your movement. If the stitches are super tiny, speed up.

• Try moving in straightish lines, wavy lines, and loops.

• To practice control, try quilting your name in cursive.

• Practice for a while until you feel confident enough to try FMQ on your collage.

• If trying FMQ on your own freaks you out, you can always invite an FMQ-experienced friend over for a "playdate."

• If you'd like to really get into free-motion quilting, a quick web search will bring up a lot of books and online classes to check out.

tip If you have experience with classic free-motion quilting motifs, then by all means go ahead and do a stipple, feathers, or loops all over the whole piece. Or you might use one free-motion quilting design on the background and something else on the face. Just make sure you make the design tight enough to stitch down all the bits!

SOMETIMES BAD IS GOOD

Are you getting nervous? Worried about ruining your piece? I have some advice for you: *Do a bad one on purpose!* Grab a scrap piece of fabric and very quickly just snip out some feature shapes—don't even worry about color or anything! It's supposed to be so terrible that you don't mind ruining it. This is different from just practicing on a plain quilt sandwich because even though you did it quickly and "bad on purpose," you will be invested more than if it were a plain test piece.

Now once you have your features glued in place, layer it with your stabilizer and stitch without fear! You may find, as most people do, that the less you worry about it, the more fun it is. Very often, people will express that approaching it with that free attitude actually improves their work.

Remember: More fretting and deliberation does not always equal a better result!

Feed-Dogs-Up Sewing

If you have an older machine that doesn't allow you to drop the feed dogs or you are not comfortable with free-motion quilting, you could choose to simply sew your face down using a regular presser foot and engaging the feed dogs as usual. This method takes a little longer than free-motion quilting since you need to stop the machine and raise and lower the presser foot when changing directions, but results will still be great.

The following options for ways to stitch down the fabric are utilitarian—they get the job of securing the collage done. Each one also creates its own look, so which you choose depends both on how secure you want the stitching to be (which depends on its intended use) and which look you prefer.

STITCHING PARALLEL LINES

With parallel-line stitching, you start on one side of the collage and work your way across to the other side, stitching across the piece and traveling down the edge to get to the next line. Make sure your lines of stitching are close enough that they catch every piece of fabric. Smaller pieces may have less stitching and larger pieces should be secured enough to withstand your project's intended use.

---

tip *I like my lines to be irregularly spaced, but if you want them evenly spaced, you can mark guides with tailor's chalk and a ruler.*

STITCHING A GRID

Sew parallel lines in one direction and then in the other, to create a grid. The grid doesn't have to be regular—it will naturally be denser in areas where you need to stitch down more pieces, like the features. If you do want the grid to be composed of evenly spaced lines, it will need to be a tight grid to ensure that all the pieces are sewn down on the features.

Parallel lines and grid stitching create a modern-looking finish.

tip *Tiny details like pupils and dots of life are usually fine with a single line of stitching going through them, but keep in mind whether your piece will be subject to handling, laundering, or wear. If so, you may opt to stitch them down more than once.*

Stitching around the Edges

Just like it sounds, for this option you stitch around and *just inside* the edges of each piece of fabric. If you stitch around each piece a few times, this will make the inevitable wonkiness of the lines look intentional. If you miss an edge, just go back over it.

While it can be done with the feed dogs engaged the "regular sewing" way, it is easier to stitch around the edges with free-motion quilting.

Stitching around the edges has more of an art quilt vibe.

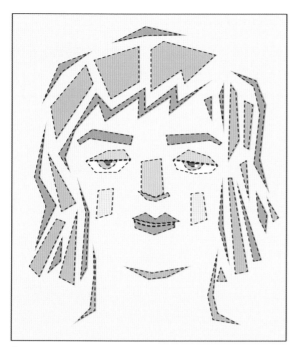

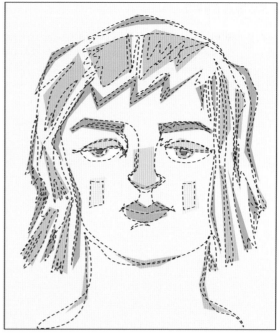

One way of stitching around edges is to secure the thread and trim after sewing each feature to avoid "travel" lines of stitching between them. This works well on simple faces without a lot of appliqué pieces filling in skin.

Another way of stitching around edges is to incorporate lines of stitching in between features. This takes some practice to make it look intentional, so it's best to start with a blending thread.

Things to think about when stitching around the edges:

- I strongly urge you to try this option on a "practice face" before committing to use it on a face that you labored over! Stitching around the edges can be tedious and takes a little practice.

- To start, use a blending thread color or invisible thread for this style of stitching. You can add some contrasting stitching over it, if desired.

- When you get to super tiny pieces, don't worry about sewing around the perimeter perfectly. Just make sure you secure the piece with stitches.

- Embrace the process. This is not needle-turn appliqué; this a raw-edge art piece!

Here are some examples to show a variety of stitch patterns and thread choices:

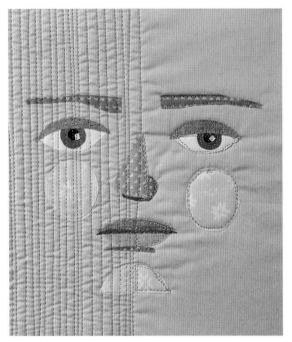

On the left, parallel-line stitching creates a subtle, modern look. On the right, the features have been stitched around the edges and the thread tied off between each feature so that no "traveling" stitches continue across the face.

On the left, I stitched around the edges of the features with blending thread and did some free-motion quilting to add textural interest and details (swirly cheek, chin, and hair). On the right, I stitched in an allover grid with blending thread. Notice how the stitching on both sides of the face is quite subtle due to the blending thread color. If I were to continue working on this piece, I would go over some details with contrasting thread to make them pop.

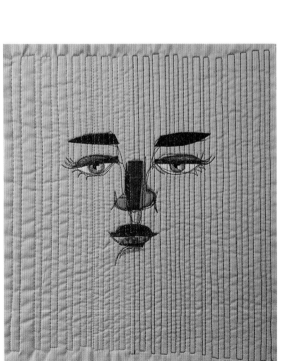

Notice how the look of the stitched parallel lines differ due to the use of blending thread on the left and contrasting thread on the right. On top of the lines, I used contrasting thread to stitch around the edges of the features to define them. Notice the "traveling" stitches between the eyebrows , eyes, nose, and mouth. I stitched over these travel lines a few times so they look intentional and fit with the rest of the stitching. If you want to experiment with travel lines, do so on a practice face that you make quickly and aren't attached to!

On this example, I stitched around the edges of the features with poly thread. If you are not confident in your stitching, poly thread is a great choice because it is very forgiving! To show this, I simply "scribbled" with thread on the right eye and to outside of it!

On this lady, I stitched around edges with contrasting thread and added eyelashes, hair, ears, earrings, and neck with free-motion stitching. Notice that on right eye and eyebrow, I tied off between them, so no travelling stitches would show; but on the rest, I incorporated traveling stitches into design. Also notice how just a few pieces of collaged fabric in the hair, along with the additional stitching, create the impression of a hairstyle.

Basic Stitching Instructions

You've created your face, layered it with an appropriate stabilizer, and chosen your thread. Let's get stitching.

If you are free-motion quilting, install the specialty foot and lower the feed dogs before you begin. If you are doing regular sewing, keep the feed dogs up (page 66) and start with the presser foot down.

Bring bobbin thread to top.

❶ With a corner of the collage under the needle, turn the handwheel toward you so the needle goes in and out of the fabric once, which pulls up the bobbin thread. Free this thread from the loop created by the top thread, and pull both threads gently to the left to keep them out of the way. This is just the same as how you would normally pull up your bobbin thread before sewing, only you are also pulling it through the fabric to be on the front instead of the back.

❷ Take a few stitches back and forth (or stitch in place) to secure the thread.

❸ Whether free-motion quilting or regular sewing, the aim is to secure all the bits of collaged fabric with stitches. You may do this in whatever way you prefer: lines, grid, around the edges, or any combination of these.

❹ When you think you are finished, run your fingers over the piece to see if any edges of the collage flip up. Secure as needed with more stitching.

❺ When finished, secure with a couple stitches back and forth (or stitch in place).

❻ Trim the thread tails.

You can always add more stitching later, even after you think the piece is "finished." I do it all the time.

tip *Once the collage is securely stitched down by machine, you may like to add hand embroidery stitches or sew on buttons or beads.*

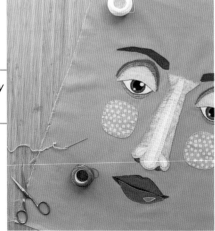

Chapter Four

Show

While I usually make just the faces and leave them as they are, you may like to turn them into some other kinds of projects. Here are a handful of ideas to get you started. I hope you'll use these examples as a springboard for your own creativity and exploration.

Pillow Cover

This pillow project is an awesome way to show off one of your best faces. Since the collage will be part of a utilitarian object, make sure it is well stitched before incorporating it into this project.

MATERIALS

Stitched face collage: Trim to 17½″ × 17½″.

Pillow form: 18″ × 18″

Fabric: ⅝ yard, prewashed, dried, and pressed (for pillow back)

Instructions

① From the pillow back fabric, cut 2 pieces 14″ × 17½″. On a single 17½″ side of each piece, fold up ½″ and press. Fold up again 2″ and press. Pin if desired and stitch ⅛″ from the inner folded edge, backstitching at the beginning and the end.

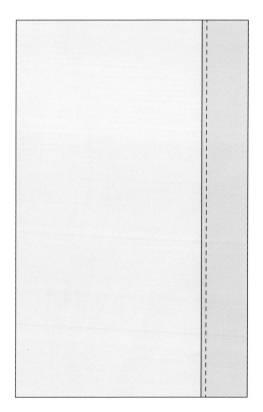

2 Edgestitch the outer fold on each piece ⅛″ from the edge. This gives the pillow opening a 2″-deep hem with an edge-stitched finish.

3 Place the collage right side up on your work surface. Place a back piece right side down, matching the raw edges and with the hemmed edge to the center. Layer the second back piece right side down, overlapping the hemmed edge and keeping the raw edges aligned on the other side. The hemmed edges will overlap about 6″ and create the "envelope" for the pillow form to go in. Make sure the pieces are all aligned and flat, and then pin in place.

4 Stitch all 4 sides with a ¼″ seam, backstitching at the beginning and the end. Pivot around the corners by lifting and lowering the presser foot when you need to change direction. Carefully clip the corners by ⅛″.

5 Turn the pillow cover right side out and gently poke the corners out using a point turner, knitting needle, or chopstick. Press the seams flat again if you like.

6 Insert the pillow form and you're done!

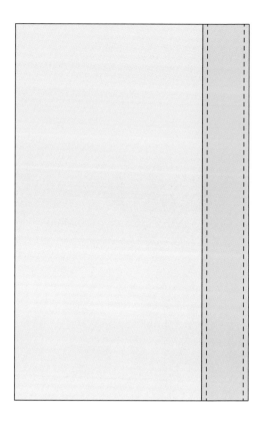

Embellished Tote

Use a face collage to add some character to a plain canvas tote. If you have a bunch of printed canvas bags (the promo kind that are given away at events), you can upcycle one by using it as the base for this project!

MATERIALS

Stitched face collage

Canvas tote bag

Measuring tape

Scissors

Lightweight fusible web: Such as HeatnBond Lite or Mistyfuse

Iron

Pressing cloth

Instructions

1 Measure the area of the bag you'd like to cover. Trim your collage to that size.

tip You can cover part of a side, a whole side, or both sides of the bag (as long as it doesn't have a pocket).

2 Cut the fusible web to the same size as the collage. Apply the fusible web to the back of the collage, according to manufacturer's instructions. If the fusible has a paper backing, remove it after it cools.

3 Lay the collage in place on the bag, adhesive side down. Lay the pressing cloth over it and press. Turn the bag inside out and press from the canvas side. Turn the bag right side out again.

4 Sew the edges of the collage to the canvas using a straight stitch. Go around a few times if you like. Trim the threads.

tip *If you have fabric paints, you could paint the rest of the bag to coordinate with your collage.*

Stretched Canvas Wall Art

Finishing your collage into this wall art project is super fast and easy but totally elevates your work. Prestretched canvases are inexpensive and can be found at your local craft shop.

MATERIALS

Stitched face collage: 11″ × 14″ on 15″ × 19″ background fabric (To avoid bulk on the back of the canvas, this project works best with a collage that has a *thin stabilizer*, such as lightweight fusible, rather than quilt batting.)

Prestretched canvas: 11″ × 14″ gallery wrapped (1½″ deep)

Staple gun: With staples

NOTE Prestretched canvas commonly comes in two different thicknesses or "profiles": regular (⅝″ deep) and gallery-wrapped (1½″ deep). The latter is a little more expensive, but it's totally worth it for the presence it creates.

---

tip *If you have a big box craft store near you, check online for a weekly coupon to print to take into the store for your purchase.*

Instructions

1 Lay the collage facedown on the table and center the canvas facedown on top. Fold the bottom edge of the fabric over the canvas and hold it in place. Staple it along this edge.

2 Gently pull the top edge of the fabric taut, fold it over the back, and secure it with staples.

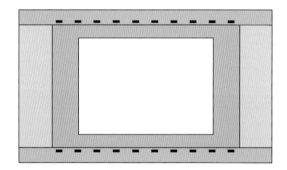

3 Starting with one corner, fold the fabric over the canvas as if you were wrapping a present or making hospital corners on a bed. Hold it in place with your fingers and look at the collage from the front to make sure the corners look crisp. Adjust it as needed and secure it with staples. Repeat this step for the remaining corners.

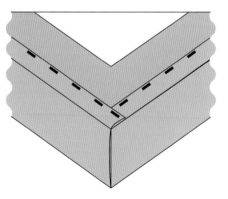

4 Finish stapling the edges along the sides. Trim the excess fabric, if desired.

Embellished Shirt

This easy embellished clothing project will make a one-of-a-kind wearable art piece. Spruce up a tired denim shirt you already have or grab one for less than ten dollars at a thrift shop.

MATERIALS

Stitched face collage:
In appropriate size to mostly fill up back of shirt

Heavyweight button-down shirt

Scissors

Lightweight fusible web:
Such as HeatnBond Lite or Mistyfuse

Iron

Pressing cloth

tips

- *This project works best with a collage that uses lightweight fusible as the stabilizer.*

- *Consider making a small related collage to sew onto the front of the shirt.*

Instructions

tip *After you cut the collage to fit the panel, if you are concerned about threads coming loose along the edges, press and sew a small hem on the piece before applying the fusible web.*

❶ Cut the fusible web to the same dimensions as the panel and apply it to the back of the collage, according to manufacturer's instructions. If the fusible has a paper backing, remove it when it cools.

❷ Open the shirt and spread it out on your ironing surface, so the back lies flat. Lay the collage in place, adhesive side down. Lay the pressing cloth over it and press it to activate the adhesive.

tip *You may need to turn up the heat setting on the iron when pressing through the front of the panel. Remember to turn it down when you press from the inside.*

❸ Turn the shirt over and press it from the inside to completely adhere the panel to the denim.

❹ From the right side, sew the edges of the collage to the shirt panel. Backstitch at the beginning and the end of the stitching to secure the thread. Trim the thread tails.

tips

- *If your machine has them, experiment with decorative stitches instead of straight stitching.*

- *If you prefer a more finished edge on your collage, you can sew ribbon or other trim on top of the edges instead of leaving them raw.*

Embellished Shirt   85

Chapter Five
Gallery of Author Work

ANCIENT PORTRAIT

- Extensive collaging on entire face and background
- Eyes, jawline, and hair outlined in thin black snippets of fabric make them stand out
- Stitched in variety of ways with tan thread: grid, tight parallel lines, and around edges of some fabric pieces

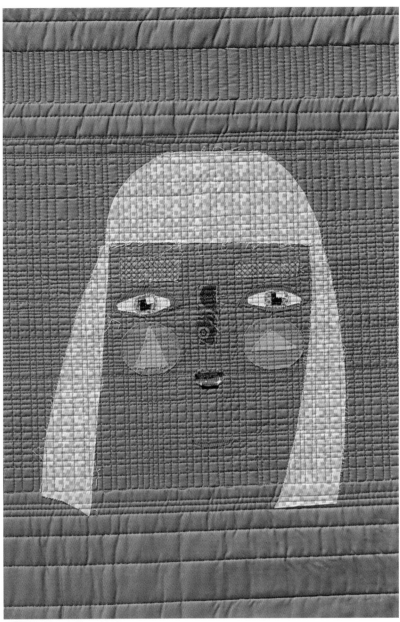

PORTLAND BLONDE

- Simple, stylized features and hair
- Rectangles for eyebrows and nose
- Triangles on cheeks
- Small, curved strip of fabric indicate chin
- Three-piece hair!
- Grid stitching

SHOT COTTON BEAUTY

- My first time using darker background fabric
- Features made mostly with shot cottons
- A lot of little pieces make up irises
- No cheeks, jawline, hair, or background design

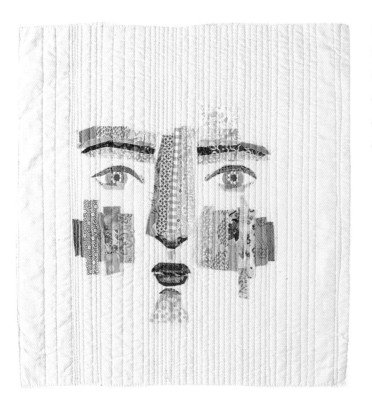

SAPPHIRE EYES

- Plain white background fabric
- Vertical straight-line stitching
- Eyes different from my usual: fussy-cut center motif instead of added pupils and highlights
- Vertical strips create nose and cheeks
- Chin indicated by stacked half-circles under mouth
- No jawline, hair, or background design

PHOTOGENIC

- Wild hair made with strips of several different fabrics, mostly similar in color, then defined by snips of darker brown
- Neck made with strips
- Nesting rows of snippets create jawline
- Plain background

 DARK DETAILS

- Tried to "ruin on purpose"!—sacrificial piece to experiment different ways to stitch over collage
- Started with tan thread to secure all pieces and then with black thread to add detail around features

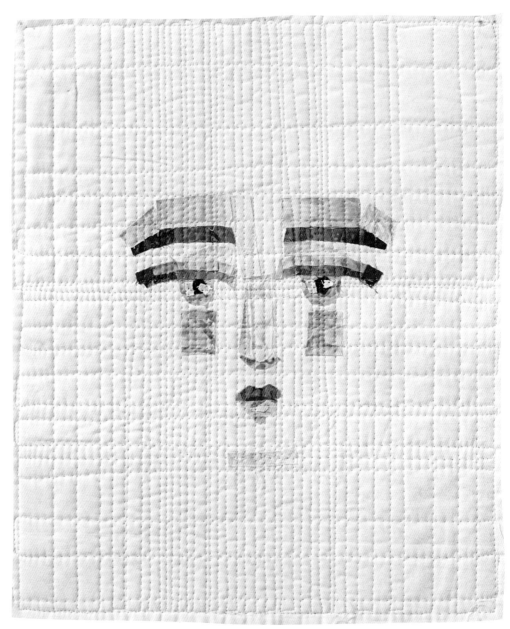

SEDONA

- Grid stitching
- Double row of fabric snippets creates eyelids
- Square cheeks
- No hair or face outline
- Fabric strip (in darker color than background) creates suggestion of chin

GUY WITH BLUE AURA

- Face collage sewn into small quilt creates striking focal point
- Improv-pieced sections frame face
- Mostly straight-line quilting complements modern look of piecing

Detail of GUY WITH BLUE AURA

- Tight grid stitching across face
- Tapered snippets of fabric define hair shape, jawline, and neck
- Radiating background made from angled fabric strips

DREAM BIG

- Moon face with encouraging words and 80s motifs create focal panel
- Straight-line stitching on bulk of quilt

Detail of DREAM BIG

- Heart between eyes and triangles on cheeks adds to whimsical look
- Yellow pupils
- Tight grid stitching across moon face

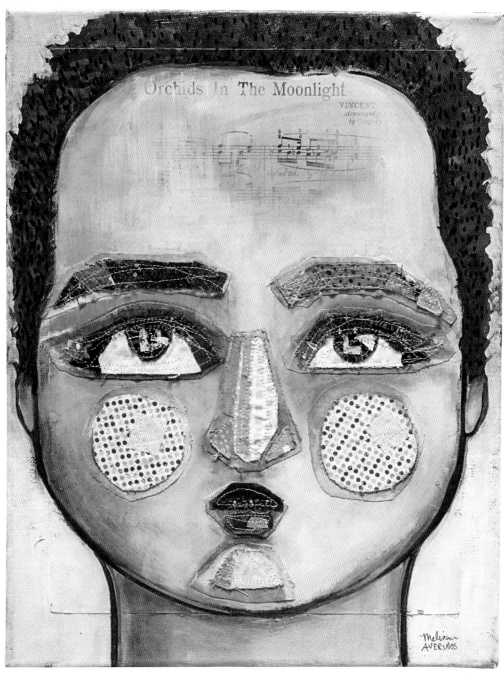

SELF PORTRAIT LOOKING UP

- Mixed media self-portrait
- On cover of *Cloth Paper Scissors* magazine (March/April 2015)
- Features made in fabric and stitched (just like the rest of examples in book), then cut out and collaged with vintage sheet music, then painted
- Mounted on stretched canvas

GIANT FABRIC SELFIE

- Large self-portrait—my first fabric face!
- Hair took forever!
- Strips of similar-colored fabric create subtle variations in skin color
- Emphasis on oversized eyes
- Whimsical background
- Outline around head transitions from red to orange and pink

Detail of GIANT FABRIC SELFIE

- A lot of different stitching
- Dark upper lip, lighter lower lip
- Lip highlights
- Many different fabrics make up each part of nose, lips, and chin

Detail of GIANT FABRIC SELFIE

- Numerous different white fabrics in whites of eyes
- Unfussy snips of fabric create variations of shadows, mid-tones, and highlights of lid
- Stitching along contours

Chapter Six
Gallery of Student Work

I love seeing how different people in class take the same instruction and create something unique. The following is a selection of student work that illustrates some of the wonderful ways people interpret all the things you just learned in this book. Some examples are stitched and bound, while others are in various stages of progress. Alongside each sample, I have listed things I want you to notice, such as how they are stitched, a unique way the student handled a feature, or the successful color choices.

UNTITLED
by Diane Hammond Wick

- Simple features
- Dark, medium, and light strips create dimension on nose
- Straight-line stitching all over and around edges of features
- Stitched circles for cheeks
- Great lip shapes

THE BLONDE and THE DUDE
by Christine Perrigo

- Pair of stylized faces on same-size background and using similar colors
- Very simple but effective features
- The L-shape line of nose
- Thin strips of fabric outline face shape and neck
- Subtle cheeks made with slightly darker fabric than background
- Straight-line stitching and around edges on faces
- Stitched free-motion swirls on background
- Texture to hair added with contrasting stitching

REDHEAD and PURPLE GIRL
by Leslie Tucker Jenison

- In progress, but clear style in faces: full lips; oversized eyes; layered brows; and wild, teardrop-shaped hair

- No jawline or chin delineated

- Limited color palette; different shades of purple and red with hints of orange and blue

CARMEN
by Laura Herron

- Multicolor, pieced background
- Abstract, angular shapes for cheeks and skin
- Snips of dark fabric on edge of upper eyelids create lash line and individual lashes
- Exaggerated dark line between lips

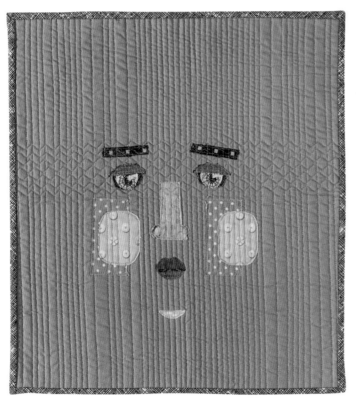

UNTITLED
by Jeri Bonser

- Very simple features on plain background
- Three-piece nose and three-piece mouth
- Layered rectangles and squarish circles create cheeks
- Straight-line stitching all over plus around edges on features

BERRIES, GREEN-HAIRED KID, and SOMEBODY'S MOTHER
by Suzanne Armstrong

- Stylized, fun, and simple
- Interesting hair, clothing, and accessories
- Thin elongated crescent shape for chin, jawline

TIA CURTIS

- Tia worked quickly, didn't agonize over choices, and made several pieces. You can see she really took to it and has her own wild style. Tia has continued to make faces for many months since the class and uses it as a reward when she finishes a deadline.

- She worked large, filling up the whole panel with the face.

- Before stitching, she layered white tulle over the panels to eliminate the concern of fabric pieces getting flipped up under the presser foot.

- Panels were quilted in white with straight-line stitching; then black thread added free-motion stitched details to the features and to create jawline and neck.

- She stitched her signature in lower right corner.

- She kept unbound, raw edges.

FAST FACE
by Tia Curtis

- Features only on background fabric
- Oversized eyes and lips
- Hair, jawline, and neck created only with contrasting thread

ROSE NOSE
by Tia Curtis

- Half of face layered in black-and-white small-scale prints
- Circle cheeks in different fabrics
- Paramecium-shaped fabrics create hair

POPCORN CHEEK
by Tia Curtis

- Different fabrics layered create skin
- Hair made from torn fabric strips

UNTITLED
by Jeri Bonser

- Several low-volume prints collaged to create textured base
- Two dark tan and one gray piece in background, contrasting with the rest, anchor face in center
- Stylized cheeks made from strips
- Simple two-piece nose
- Stitching around edges secure features to background

LET YOUR HAIR DOWN
by Stella Singleton

- I love how Stella makes hair!
- Slightly wavy strips in several shades of brown make convincing long hairstyle with side-swept bangs
- Diagonal straight-line stitching in gray blends with face (You barely notice that it contrasts with hair.)

TOPKNOT
by Stella Singleton

- Used different dark brown fabrics in very subtle prints to make topknot hairstyle; added hair highlights and interest with slightly brighter fabric that has built-in color variation (Really awesome fabric choice!)

SORTA SELF-PORTRAIT
by Cheryl Arkison

- Face on very light base; dark fabric strips at lash lines help make whites of eyes stand out

- Mix of black and brown fabrics in subtle prints, creating shape of hair

- Stitched matchstick, straight lines in white thread blend on face (Barely noticeable contrast on hair.)

LISTEN
by Veronica Hofman-Ortega

- Excellent example of filling in entire head and neck with fabric bits
- Features quite simple, but strong overall effect
- Face stitched in simple grid pattern
- Awesome background treatment—variation of small free-motion quilting motifs surrounding the word *listen*
- Wide blue border surrounding white panel, pieced and seamed to face panel make piece larger
- Bound like regular quilt

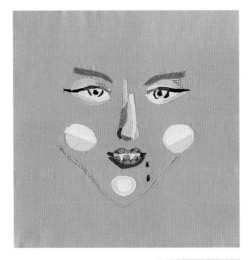

YUM #1
by Lauren Hawley

- I love that Lauren turned her lady into a vampire!
- A lot of different pieces make up eyes
- Dark lines around irises to add more contrast so they pop against white of eye
- Zigzag and straight lines of stitching around and within features
- Combination of circle and strip cheeks
- Chin created with layers of similar-color circles

RED HOT BUNS
by Tessa Williams

- Hair made from almond shapes plus buns with curved highlight strips
- Very simple features
- Irises made from fussy-cut fabric

FEELING BLUE
by Cathy McQuitty-Dreiling

- Made in all shades of blue to create harmonious look
- Features made from layering light, medium, and dark blue / aqua fabrics
- Polka-dot cheeks, again in same color family
- Finished with hand-sewn blanket stitch around every piece
- Thread colors to match each fabric stitched down
- Additional embroidery in and under eyes

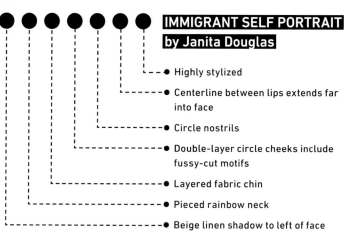

IMMIGRANT SELF PORTRAIT
by Janita Douglas

- Highly stylized
- Centerline between lips extends far into face
- Circle nostrils
- Double-layer circle cheeks include fussy-cut motifs
- Layered fabric chin
- Pieced rainbow neck
- Beige linen shadow to left of face

- Simple, elongated shapes for ears
- Thin strips of brown fabric outline sides of face
- Original background fabric cut away and head layered onto pieced background
- Stitched with straight lines in background; free-motion around edges and within face elements
- Signed with stitching on right side of neck

FACE #1
by Angela Garrison

- Started on subtly textured, almost-white fabric
- Blue background added around head and neck
- Variety of subtle, low-volume prints collaged onto face create interest
- Hair created in single fabric
- Snips of black added to outer corner of eyes give impression of eyelashes, creating more feminine look
- Simple, subtle shadow for nose
- Highlights on lips
- Shadow under chin creates jawline
- Stitched with straight lines on background, face, and around edges on hair

THE DUDE
by Diane Hammond Wick

- Painterly quality
- Background grading from light to dark
- Nonrealistic colors create realistic-looking and captivating face
- Half-ovals for ears
- Facial hair and bold brows "masculinize" basic face
- Shadows and highlights: overall, face darker on left and lighter on right
- Strip of dusty plum fabric creates shadow of brim on forehead
- Stitched in purple thread with straight lines and stitched around edges on features; more detail added with black thread

ELAINE WICK POPLIN

- Elaine is a precision-piecing math teacher who took to the technique as if she were a painter!

- All three of her pieces have subtle highlights and shadows but overall are darker on the left side, lighter on the right.

- Made using batik fabrics.

THE BARONESS VON BROCCOLI by Elaine Wick Poplin

- Crazy hair made of circles (inspiration for naming the project!)
- Downward tilt of eyes at outer corners give her sad or pensive look
- Contrasting stitching around edges and all over face
- Blending thread for free-motion swirls stitched all over background

MAY THE ODDS BE EVER IN YOUR FAVOR! and ICE PRINCESS by Elaine Wick Poplin

- Pair of faces
- Dense free-motion stitching all over
- Collaged backgrounds with fabrics in same color with slight variation from light to dark
- Whimsical, stylized hair
- Face, neck, and hair completely filled in with fabric
- Subtle shadow under nose, mouth, and jawline
- Subtle highlights and shadows: left side of each face made with slightly darker fabrics than each right side

SELF-PORTRAIT
by Michelle Engel Bencsko
and
QUILTED HEAD (AFTER HAUSMANN)
by Andrew Bencsko

- Magic happened when this married pair of artists took my class together.
- Self-portraits with stylized, graphic vibe
- Large pieces of fabric create face and neck (also hair, in Michelle's case)
- Solid fabrics in bold colors and abstract shapes fill in skin
- Variations of lighter and darker fabrics creating highlights and shadows on faces
- Light on details
- Modern look

About the Author

Melissa Averinos has been painting, collaging, and sewing since her teens and has always focused on faces. She is a fabric designer, a painter, and an award-winning quilter. She is also a regular contributor to quilt and craft magazines.

Melissa travels nationally to teach her signature class "Making Faces with Melissa" at quilt shops, guilds and events. Her approach to teaching is lighthearted, fun, and inclusive. Even non-artists feel comfortable experimenting in her workshops.

Melissa loves Atomic Fireballs, unicorns, rust, yoga, thrift shopping, and summertime. She loves heartfelt hugs and is a good listener. She lives on Cape Cod with her adorable husband, Stuart, and their two golden retrievers, Max and Beau.

FOLLOW MELISSA ON SOCIAL MEDIA:

Website: melissaaverinos.com

Instagram: @melissaaverinos
(Share photos of your collages on Instagram! Use the hashtag #makingfaceswithmelissa.)

Pinterest: /melissaaverinos

Facebook: /yummygoods

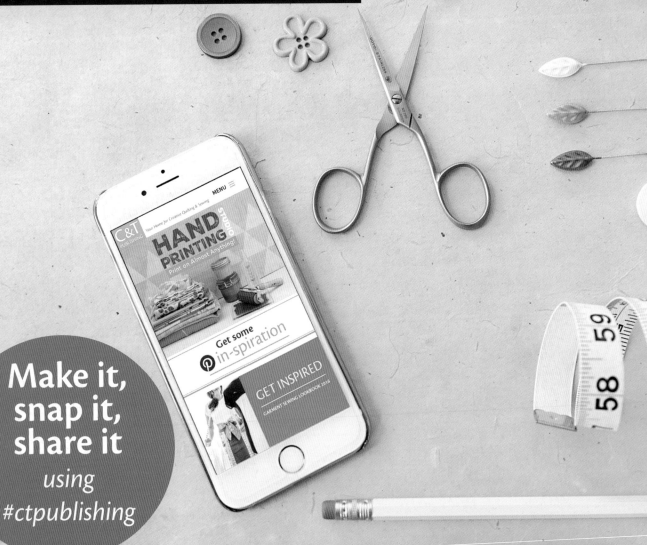